Light My Candle

Given to

_____

From

_____

Date

_____

My prayer for you

_____

_____

_____

For thou wilt *Light My Candle:*
the LORD *my God will enlighten my darkness.*   *Psalm 18:28*

Light My Candle

Prayers in the Darkness of Miscarriage

–Stephanie J. Leinbach–

Light My Candle
© 2011 by Stephanie J. Leinbach

All Scripture quotations are taken from the King James Version of the Bible.

ISBN 13: 978-0615-43615-9
ISBN 10: 0-61543615-3

Cover Design:
Joseph Ebersole / Illustra Graphics
Myerstown, PA (717) 679-2390

For questions, comments, or to purchase
additional copies of this book, please contact:
Candlewood Publications
521 Cooney Lane
Altoona, PA 16601
(814) 201-2836
lightmycandle@abcmailbox.net

Printed by:

Carlisle Printing
OF WALNUT CREEK LTD
800.927.4196

Dedication

To the women in my life,

who helped me become the woman I am.

And to Linford, the man in my life,

who has loved me through it all.

Acknowledgements

I am profoundly grateful to those who helped make this book possible. There are many who contributed in numerous ways, but my dear husband deserves my warmest thanks. Linford, you admit to being unable to make heads or tails of my poetry, but without your encouragement, this book would never have happened. You have remained supportive even though you had to live with me throughout the labor and delivery of this book. Blessed am I among women to be your wife!

To those who provided valuable reviewing and editing assistance, my deep gratitude: Lois Heller, my mother, but most of all my friend; Lucille Leinbach, who raised the man I love and did an excellent job of it; Lenna Martin, who knows the pain of empty places; Cassondra Heller, sister extraordinaire; Sheryl Leinbach and Charlene Leinbach, sisters-in-law and sisters-of-the-heart; Joyce Witmer, the one whose enthusiasm planted the seed that became this book and my go-to person for various conundrums; Joy Martin, who watered the seed and spared not the fertilizer of encouragement.

I also appreciate the patience of the experts with this novice to the publishing world. Joseph Ebersole did an excellent job of capturing the intensity and emotion of this book in the creation of the cover. Aaron Hershberger gave the encouragement I needed to prevent me from giving up. He also took the time to answer all my questions about the publishing process. Rosetta, a mere acknowledgement falls short of expressing my appreciation for all that you've done to help make *Light My Candle* shine. Thank you for your unending patience with the "details."

I am reminded by the sweet miracle of life around me and within my heart that I owe my greatest debt to our Lord, the Light and Saviour of the world. Without His love, His salvation, His gift of life, I am nothing. All honor and glory belong to Him alone.

Contents

Introduction

I never intended for you to read these poems. What is contained on these pages is my private response to a personal grief. I wrote out of necessity and desperation, in order to cope with the tumult of emotions brought on by the devastation of miscarriage. I remember, just hours after we learned our first baby no longer lived, sitting down and writing *Lines of Loss*. From somewhere deep within, words came and phrases formed; I could barely write fast enough. I grieved through my pen in the days to come. So often, I grieved alone.

This aloneness, at a time when I was already bereft and empty, created in me a desire to connect with other women who also had experienced miscarriage. As I encountered those taking a similar journey of loss, I shared some of my poetry in the hope it might encourage them. These women in turn encouraged me to do something productive with my poems, but it wasn't until after my second miscarriage that I was willing to share such an intensely personal side of myself on this scale.

The story of my journey with miscarriage is included in this book. I tell it to you in order to present the setting in which these poems were written. I do not wish to capitalize on my pain or loss, neither do I wish to hold up my experience as more difficult or more painful than someone else's. In some respects, I have not lost very much, but we are not able to measure and judge another's pain as more or less than our own. God gives each individual the grace she needs to endure the experiences unique to her.

Please take these poems as an unfolding story, a journey through the stages of grief. There are poems in this book that end with an unresolved issue: anger, bitterness, or self-pity. Healing takes time; it was not all accomplished while writing a few short lines. May you see and experience the process of healing taking place as you read through these pages.

Do not expect to be able to identify with every poem in this book. Our journeys and perspectives are all unique. When I received the reviews from the women I asked to read over this manuscript, I was fascinated - and somewhat dismayed - to realize that a poem liked by one woman was disliked by another. There were some personal favorites of mine interpreted differently than I intended. As an author, it is scary to think that I could - and probably will - be misunderstood. If something does not connect with you, it is confirmation that we are all different. What was in my journey may not be in yours.

A brief note on the style of poetry I use: most of these poems are free verse, thoughts written in a poetical fashion without being confined to rhyme or rhythm. I was unable to express myself adequately within the rigid standards of traditional rhyme-and-rhythm poetry, so I used this less common style. I believe you will find it easier to read than traditional verse.

I pray these words may provide a sense of companionship, comfort, and hope to those of you on a journey you did not wish to take. May you find peace in the midst of grief and an awareness of our loving Father's presence as you walk this dark path. To those who have never lost a child through miscarriage, it is my hope that you will have a greater understanding of the impact it may have on a woman's heart. Most of all, may these words glorify the Healer of broken hearts.

A Cry to the Creator

Hear my cry, O God; attend unto my prayer.

From the end of the earth will I cry unto thee,

when my heart is overwhelmed:

lead me to the rock that is higher than I.

Psalm 61:1-2

prayers in the midst of darkness

Looking back, I find it remarkable how easily I embraced my first pregnancy without a thought that I could be opening my arms to pain and heartbreak. I was pregnant! Dizzy with anticipation and happiness, I never considered any possibility other than the sweet surety that in less than nine months, we would be holding our baby.

It was a staggering blow when the bleeding began. We contacted the midwife who told us to come in for blood work. She drew a blood sample, the first in a series of tests, to measure the amount of hCG, the pregnancy hormone, in my blood. In a viable pregnancy, this hormone count doubles every 24-36 hours.

The possibility of losing our baby left me feeling dazed and helpless. I was seven weeks pregnant, beginning to suffer the pangs of morning sickness. I wept; I prayed; I begged God to let me keep my baby, as the bleeding continued over the next few days. The results from the blood test came back; my hormone count was high enough to suggest that everything could be fine. I was scheduled for a second test to see if the count had risen sufficiently for an active pregnancy.

Four days after the bleeding started, it stopped. Our hopes rose. But that evening, following an episode of severe abdominal pain, we went to the emergency room for answers. Pain and spotting in early pregnancy can sometimes be an indication of an ectopic pregnancy.

I remember the doctor: her kind face, her gentle hands, and the obvious swelling of her own pregnancy. We discussed the circumstances that brought us in that night, and I watched her as she watched the monitor during the ultrasound. Our eyes met as she turned to me.

"I'm so sorry…." The warning signs had been there. The possibilities of miscarriage had been presented to us. We knew the facts, but my heart was not prepared for the shattering words of the doctor.

"The baby is there, but there is no heartbeat."

Somehow, my heart managed to keep beating as it broke into a thousand pieces. I looked at where her baby resided so safely, a little heartbeat that had not stopped. I wanted to scream out my pain, but there were no words in me. I could only lean into my husband's shoulder and cry.

"The pregnancy is over. Your body has already begun the process of miscarriage." No matter how gently she said it, the doctor's words still cut to my very core.

So…we went home to have a miscarriage.

Light My Candle

For thou wilt light my candle:
the LORD my God will enlighten my darkness. Psalm 18:28

Lord,
  all is darkness,
    lifeless,
      cold and silent
        within me.
The light that flickered and shone
      for so short a time
    has been cruelly snuffed out.
I am left alone,
  weeping in this black night
    of miscarriage.
An emptiness envelops me;
  a life is over,
      finished,
        done.
I'm drained and broken,
    crying in the dark.
I should be surrounded
    by light and happiness
      and certainty.
Instead, I clutch
    with despairing hands
  at dreams that dance
      beyond my reach.
Lord,
  in this dreadful darkness
    of loss…
  in this tearful night
    of grief…
Light my candle.
    Lighten my darkness.
  Give me enough light
so that I may clearly see
    You
  in the darkness
    beside me.

Lines of Loss

He healeth the broken in heart, and bindeth up their wounds. Psalm 147:3

Oh, Father God,
    Maker of worlds and stars,
sometimes the smallest miracle
            is the greatest of them all.
For too short a time, I knew inside
        a wonder too great to comprehend;
    for too brief a time, I carried within
        the tiniest wonder of all –
            too tiny, too tender
            for this big, tough world.
And looking down on the two of us,
    You knew it was time –
            my baby's time –
        to come home.
So precious was he in Your eyes,
        You could not wait for man's allotted time to pass.
    Your time is not our time, Father,
        so we do not understand.
And when my arms, my empty arms,
        ache with the weight of my baby's absence,
    give me the strength to grieve,
        the strength to cry,
            the strength to laugh,
        when a baby passing by
        smiles at his brand new world –
        a world my baby will not ever know.
Help me to understand
    my baby has gone on before me –
        oh, why should children lead the way for us? –
    and happiness and joy surround each child
            You have welcomed home.
God, hold my baby's hand;
        I cannot reach that far.
    Take him in Your arms,
            this child of my heart.

An Empty Motherhood

As one whom his mother comforteth, so will I comfort you... Isaiah 66:13a

Oh, God,
   I am a mother,
           aren't I?
Even though my child
   lived but weeks
      beneath my heart
   and now dwells
        within Your arms,
that still makes me a mother,
         right?
I am a mother who
   never held her little one,
      never rocked her baby to sleep,
      never whispered a prayer at a bedside.
I never heard my baby cry
      because my baby has gone
   to a place of no tears,
          no pain,
     not even a prayer,
        for God is right there.
I can only cry,
        and hurt,
   and pray.
God, I know You're here,
   but I wish I could see You,
     as my baby does.
I am a mother –
      a mother without a baby;
   I must pray for strength
        to move on.
I'm letting my baby
      rest in Your arms.

Thank You, Lord,
    that there's room enough
       for me there, too.

Interior Design

Why is my pain perpetual?... Jeremiah 15:18a

Oh, God,
>   why don't You just pack up the pain
>   and move it out of my life?

But if You won't,
>   then help me find a suitable place
>   to put it,
>   a place where pain
>   is balanced with acceptance,
>   and grief
>   is enhanced with growth –
>with You in the center of it all,
>   in focus.
>   You need to be the Focus.

Help me put my pain in a place
>   where I can get used to it,
>   but don't constantly see it.

God,
>   why does there have to be
>   a place for pain?

Bitter Sweet

Wherefore is light given to him that is in misery,
and life unto the bitter in soul. Job 3:20

I feel so hollow,
        so empty
    inside.
There had been
        so much life,
        so much potential
    within me.

I feel robbed
    of my greatest
        mission:
        bringing new life
    into this world.
        Oh, God,
        how
        could You
        do this
            to me?

I feel the warmth,
        the whisper
    of Your presence.
Oh, God,
        why does it take
    the greatest pain
        to make You
    so real,
        so wonderful
        to me?

Lord,
    I come to You
    with this great
        emptiness.
I realize now
    my greatest mission:
        coming to You
        empty,
    so I can be
    filled to overflowing
        with Your love,
        and yes,
            even joy.

Empty Arms

For I the LORD thy God will hold thy right hand, saying unto thee,
Fear not; I will help thee. Isaiah 41:13

Oh, God,
    my arms are so empty,
        but for these broken dreams.

They are much heavier to carry
        than the sweet weight
    my child would've been.

I wish,
    I long,
        I pray,
    for something…
  something to hold onto,
    someone to rest in my arms,
      trusting me,
        loving me,
    depending on me,
  simply because he is
    my child.
Nothing on earth,
    within my power,
  could harm that
    little one
      in my arms.

But, God,
    my arms are so empty.

And then,
    Lord,
    I hear You say,
"Child,
  your arms are empty,
    but so are Mine.
Your heart is designed

to come to Me with your great emptiness
and rest in My arms.
Nothing, dear child,
on heaven or earth,
could harm you then.

Where are you,
sad child of Mine?
Come to Me,
with your broken dreams
and your empty arms.
I long for you,
just as you long for the baby
I welcomed home.
Your arms are empty,
but, child,
come rest in Mine."

A Cry to the Creator

Unto thee will I cry, O LORD my rock; be not silent to me:
lest, if thou be silent to me, I become like them that go down
into the pit. Psalm 28:1

You spoke,
    and the world was.
You spoke,
       and it was very good.

Lord,
  why didn't You speak to my child
        words of life,
      words of comfort,
    bidding him to stay
        with me awhile?
You are the sustainer of life;
    why did You fail to sustain
  that which was so precious to me?
Surely You have everything
       You need or want;
    why did You want my child, too?

You spoke,
    and the sun shone.
You spoke,
      and the birds sang.

Lord,
  why didn't You speak to me
    in my hour of loss,
        words of explanation,
      words of justification,
    bidding me to understand
      why You took my baby away?
You are the source of joy;
    why have You taken mine?
There are millions singing praises
       around Your throne;
    did You really need one more?

You spoke,
    but today the pain speaks louder.
You spoke,
    but I hear only the echo…

                echo…

                        echo…

            of my falling tears.

Bedtime Prayer

Yet the LORD will command his lovingkindness in the daytime,
and in the night his song shall be with me,
and my prayer unto the God of my life. Psalm 42:8

Lord,
    I come to You
  in the midnight hour,
      when the distance
    between earth and heaven
      is not quite so far.
In the cool, still darkness
        of this earth,
  it might be possible –
      if everything could just
       be very, very quiet –
    to hear the angels sing.
But the world keeps turning,
      and life keeps on going,
  and we can never quite
close the gap between
      earth and heaven.
But, Lord,
  (this is what I stayed up
     to talk to You about)
  I find the gap in my heart
     between earth and heaven
   a lot smaller these days.
Do you remember, Lord,
     not too long ago,
  a tiny, tiny little baby
    that came to live with You?
I don't know what
   that baby looked like –
     don't even know if
    that baby was a boy or a girl –
so I hope You know which one
   I am talking about.
Lord, that baby was mine.
     And now my baby is Yours.

Do You know how much that hurts?
I hope Somebody was there
            to welcome my baby home.
He was so small, so tiny;
        it would be easy to miss him.
I can't bear to think of him
        lost, lonely, and scared.
    I'm sure You took him in Your arms,
            because I know You love children.
I miss my baby,
            the baby I've never held.
I find my thoughts drifting
        heavenward throughout the day,
        wondering what sights
            my child is seeing.
I even feel slightly envious,
    of my child, and of You, Lord,
    for You dwell with
    the first child of my womb,
            and my child has walked
    the streets of glory before I have.
            That doesn't seem right, Lord.
Children shouldn't precede
        their parents into eternity.
    It hurts too much.

Closing my eyes,
    I see a child laughing,
                running,
            playing,
    in the green meadows of Glory.
It's an earth-painted picture, Lord,
            but let me fall asleep
        with my child's laughter
still ringing in my mind's ear,
        and the longing in my mother-heart
        to see my child someday.

Questions for a Sovereign God

My God, my God, why hast thou forsaken me?... Psalm 22:1a

Where are You, God,
 when babies die and children cry?
Where are You, God,
 when broken dreams around me lie?
Where are You, God,
 when all I see is emptiness and pain?
Where are You, God,
 when it seems the sun won't shine again?
I look around; You can't be found;
 my heartache grows; my tears still flow;
 God, do You even know?
Then through the mist of pain and tears,
 a still, small voice, so soft, I hear:
 "My child, I am here.
This all fits in My master plan;
 I know you do not understand,
 but still I mold you, gently hold you,
 keep you safe within My care.
Your world has death and tears and pain,
 and always will, for sin is there.
 But, My child, don't you know?
The more you suffer there below,
 the more you long for what awaits,
 just beyond these pearly gates.
Did you forget I'm in control?
Who died for you to save your soul?
 You are so sad, dear child of Mine,
 but your sorrow brings to mind
 that someday there will be no tears,
 and I am waiting for you here.
It's one more reason you should long
 to stand among the heavenly throng.
'Where are You, God?' you ask of Me;
 did you ask Me where you should be?
I want you here where tears won't be;
 your pain is turning you to Me."

Offering or Sacrifice?

(Offering: to present for acceptance)
(Sacrifice: loss, deprivation)

Honour the LORD with thy substance,
and with the firstfruits of all thine increase. Proverbs 3:9

Lord,
   I have always tried
       to offer the best of what I have
         back to You,
     like the Israelites of old.
I am sure
      their hearts were filled with joy
    as they came to Your house
      laden with the best,
        the brightest,
          the most perfect –
            their firstfruits –
        to offer to You.
But, Lord,
   I have given to You
       the Firstfruit of my womb;
    I have relinquished my earthly hold
        on my sweet, tiny firstborn.
I have accepted the fact
    that my child wasn't made to live
        anywhere but heaven.
Lord,
    where is the joy?
I want to *give* my baby
     to Your eternal care,
      an innocent soul
    for Your heavenly kingdom,
        an offering of the Firstfruits.

But, Lord,
    why does it feel like a sacrifice?

Depression

Why art thou cast down, O my soul? and why art thou disquieted
within me? hope thou in God: for I shall yet praise him,
who is the health of my countenance, and my God. Psalm 42:11

Lord,
    at times like this,
  I feel like I have
   poured out my grief
     and am wallowing in it.
I can't get away from the loss,
    the emptiness,
     the tears bottled up inside.
Time has passed;
  surely there should be
     an end to grief.
Instead, here I am,
     with my broken heart,
   feeling the shards of loss
    slicing into my soul.
There doesn't seem to be
    any way out.

Today, it finally hit me.
   In a way,
  it was a relief to recognize it:
    Depression.
  The mood swings,
    the weariness,
      the insecurities,
   the fears,
     the loneliness…
  Depression.
I have not been purposely
  dwelling on my loss;
    it just rises up,
 larger than life,
    to confront me with
  what should have been.

Lord,
   forgive me if this is my fault.
I am confused and afraid,
        but I shore up the barriers
   and sally forth to say to others,
      "I am doing well."

It is only at times like this,
   when everything is too big
         to hold inside,
      that I come face to face
         with the deep wounds
      left by loss and grief.
There is an internal balance
               thrown off center
      by my miscarriage,
   a sensor triggered
      by the interruption of death.
I cannot reach inside
            and change it.
It is an intrinsic part of me,
      as much as my baby was.
   And so I am caught,
         between life and death,
   my body on a time-clock
      that has already broken.
Forgive me, Lord,
   if my emotions get
         the best of me.
      This, too, shall pass.
Just give me the grace to endure
   and the strength to face
      my weakness,
         and,
         someday,
         my future.

A Mother's Prayer

I will both lay me down in peace, and sleep:
for thou, Lord, only makest me dwell in safety. Psalm 4:8

Now I lay me down to sleep…
but I lie awake,
thinking of the little one that sleeps
an eternal sleep
till Jesus calls.
There is a maternal rhythm
to my heart
that has me restless and disturbed.

I pray Thee, Lord, Thy child to keep…
but, Lord, there is a tiny soul
that slipped away
out of fragile moorings,
a tiny soul that You now keep.
The memory of that little absence
keeps me awake tonight.

Guard me safely through the night…
(oh, Lord, You know all the stars
by name and number –
are You counting my tears?)
There is a little one
who will never be afraid of the dark
for he has gone
to a place of eternal Light.
I lie here staring at the ceiling,
counting all the milestones
I missed
and the memories that will never be.

And keep me safe till morning light…
You have taken the sweet soul of my child
in Your arms;
the Light that shines upon him will never set.
In the long hours of darkness

that knowledge presents
a ray of light.
My baby is safely home,
kept in Your care.
Lord, is that not the answer
to a mother's greatest prayer?

But, Lord, my weary heart longs for rest,
and tomorrow looms around the corner...
help me find sleep...
lay me down to sleep...
in peace...
help me trust in Your unfailing love...

In Jesus' name...
and in His arms...

Amen.

Treasure in Heaven

But lay up for yourselves treasures in heaven, where neither moth nor rust
doth corrupt, and where thieves do not break through nor steal:
For where your treasure is, there will your heart be also. Matthew 6:20-21

Lord,
        in Your Word,
    You ask us to lay up
            our treasure in heaven.
I have,
        Lord;
                I have.
The greatest treasure
        a human heart can hold
    has been given over to Your care.
But sometimes,
        (I'm sorry, Lord!)
    I feel like You are the thief
            that breaks through and steals.
Remind me, Lord,
            that my precious treasure
    will achieve a more beautiful
                luster and shine
    beneath Your tender care and protection
                than it would here on earth.
Help me remember
            I have given to You
    a treasure of more value
                than the whole world could hold.
I have given You my child,
        created in love,
                nurtured in hope,
        mourned in loss.

For where your treasure is, there will your heart be also.

It is,
        Lord;
            it is.

Why?

*Will the LORD be pleased with thousands of rams, or with ten thousands
of rivers of oil? shall I give my firstborn for my transgression,
the fruit of my body for the sin of my soul? Micah 6:7*

Why?
    I have come to You,
        over and over,
      bringing this question.
Once more
    my feet find the path,
  worn and tearstained,
  bearing this word:
    why?
Have I fallen so short
    of who I should be
  that You felt the need
    to remind me Who is in control?
Have You taken
    the fruit of my body
  for the sin of my soul?
I know You love me,
    but right now,
  I feel chastised and abandoned.
    Why?
This is a familiar path,
  but I stumble and fall
    at Your feet,
      where all questions belong.
Lord,
  help me let my questions there.
Help me get to my feet
  and find a new path
    to You...
      to a new day.

Heartcry

In my distress I called upon the LORD, and cried to my God:
and he did hear my voice out of his temple, and my cry did enter
into his ears. 2 Samuel 22:7

You're the Maker of all,
    so why didn't You try
to step in and stop
    our baby from dying?
There are so many tears
      and so many whys;
where are You, God,
    when an innocent dies?
Forgive me, oh, Lord,
    I'm angry again;
it doesn't seem fair,
    and I don't understand.
Death is our curse
    when we live on this earth,
but our baby was taken
    before the time of his birth.
Oh, God, You're our Father,
    You've created all things;
I am broken inside,
    no song left to sing.
Reach down, oh, so gently,
    past all this great pain,
and take my heart pieces –
    make me whole again.
Remind me our little one's
    safe in Your care;
the first breath he took
    was celestial air.
Heal this anger and pain
    and my shattered heart;
walk with me, Father,
    I am lost in the dark.

Letters to Heaven

And God shall wipe away all tears from their eyes;

and there shall be no more death, neither sorrow, nor crying,

neither shall there be any more pain:

for the former things are passed away. Revelation 21:4

a mother's longing for her child

We went home to have a miscarriage, but it didn't turn out to be that simple. The bleeding had stopped. We went for more blood work. To our surprise, my hCG levels had climbed. Apparently, my body had not yet figured out that our baby had died.

More blood work. The bleeding began again. Morning sickness was taking its toll. Another call from the midwife told us that my hormones were still climbing. I felt very pregnant, but the facts contradicted my feelings.

This continued for six weeks. I would start bleeding, but it would stop after a few days. I was the only one, of course, able to monitor the whole process, but at what point did the bleeding indicate the miscarriage had actually occurred? We discussed our options. Should we do a D&C? We had chosen to use the non-interference method, but this was getting ridiculous.

During this time, my mind could not handle the roller coaster ride of emotions, so it went into hibernation. Reality just slid by without touching me. I felt frozen inside.

Six weeks after our hospital visit, I was bleeding again. It was a little heavier than usual, but by now I had become used to it and didn't worry very much. It continued for three days, turning increasingly heavier. By the third day, I was wondering how much blood one person could lose without it becoming dangerous. That evening, I passed out from blood loss.

I don't remember much about the next few hours. Bits and pieces of images rise up in my mind, but nothing is coherent. My husband doesn't like to talk about that night. I scared him half to death by fainting in his arms, and he has no desire to relive anything that happened in the hours following.

I was rushed to the hospital where they took me to surgery for a D&C. I remember waking up in the recovery room and being so horribly cold. Every single muscle in my body hurt. Linford was allowed to see me for a few minutes. He was almost as pale as I was. Poor man! He hadn't asked for this.

Our baby was gone – really, truly gone – this time. I could have been gone as well. I couldn't muster the strength to cry about either at the moment.

I spent the remainder of the night in a semi-private room while Linford was permitted to catch a few hours of sleep on a sofa in a nearby lounge. It was a long and horrible night. The woman sharing my room was in severe pain and moaned for hours before falling asleep. I was in pain as well and very restless. It was getting close to morning when a nurse came in and gave me some medication that allowed me to finally fall asleep.

The next morning, a doctor came by and recommended a blood transfusion before they released me. They were not willing to let me go home until I was able to walk down the hall with assistance. I was weak as a newborn kitten. Sitting up exhausted me. We agreed. We wanted to go home.

Sometime that morning Linford came in and told me that a couple we knew had just had their first child, a boy. He was born during the night, just down the hall from my room. We cried then, the significance of our loss contrasting so clearly against their joy. It was in that moment that my emotions came out of hibernation. The pain so long held back poured in. Our loss was now definite, clear, and unquestionable. I had miscarried our first child. We were back where we had started, only with broken hearts.

Sometime after this experience, I was researching miscarriage and found some information we should have known sooner. It stated that the longer a woman carries a baby that has died, the greater her risk of hemorrhaging becomes. Perhaps you think we should have opted for medical intervention before it became dangerous. You are right; we should have, but we were young and ignorant of the risks we were taking. I passed out ten minutes after my husband got home from work. If it had happened during the day while I was alone… Let our experience be a warning: if you are losing excessive amounts of blood, please seek medical advice and attention without delay.

The Curtain Between

For thou hast delivered my soul from death:
wilt not thou deliver my feet from falling, that I may walk
before God in the light of the living? Psalm 56:13

The night passes by,
    but barely,
   in infinite slowness.
Surrounded by the dark shadows
  caused by loss of dreams and blood,
      I drift,
    somewhere between
        asleep and awake.
I am aware
   of a great emptiness
    within,
  as if everything inside
    has been torn loose
      and cast aside.
   And the pain.
I am always aware
  of the pain.

On the other side of the curtain,
   a woman moans unceasingly;
  it sounds as if she sings
    her death song.

I stare into the nothingness
  of this hospital room,
   longing for sleep,
    for forgetfulness,
   for escape from the dirge
  on the other side of the curtain.

I think of a different curtain
  stretched between our world
    and another,

a boundary between time and space,
and eternity.
I think of the tiny soul
too big for its mortal bindings,
which broke free and slipped through
that curtain.

Yet here I lie,
unable to reach across that Great Divide
and grasp to me that precious soul.
Never have I felt so helpless.

I turn my head
to stare at the shadowy barrier
hanging between my bed and another.
By that bed,
perhaps,
Death waits for yet one more soul.

But on the other side
of that eternal curtain,
only life awaits.

That thought alone
is what gets me through
the night.

A Letter to Heaven

*… can I bring him back again? I shall go to him, but he
shall not return to me. 2 Samuel 12:23b*

Dear Baby,
child of mine,
you may not know me,
but I am your mother.
I carried you within me,
nourished you,
cherished you,
anticipated you,
but God had other plans.

Oh,
sweet little one,
you go to God
untouched,
unscarred,
unblemished
by this cruel world.

You will never know
of pain,
or crying,
or loss.
You will only know eternal love
within your Father's care.
You go with no regrets,
and, oh, so brief a history,
a story barely told.

My baby,
my little stranger,
I will never know you.
You lived and played
and cried and laughed,
but only in my dreams.

Although you dwelt beneath my heart,
    you were never in my arms.

How can I miss you?
    You were barely here.
How can I wish you to return?
    You're so happy over there.

You stole into my life so softly,
    taking up residence there,
  and slipped away as softly,
    leaving in your wake
      blood,
          pain,
             tears.
I miss you.
    I wish you were here.
But seeing there is no way
    to bring you back from where you are
        into my arms,
    baby of mine,
someday I'm coming home
    to see you.

Little One Loved

God's finger touched him, and he slept. -Tennyson

Little one loved,
  we wanted you so very much,
even though we never touched
    your tender skin,
    or held your hand.
You were in our hearts,
  little one loved.

Little one loved,
  we never saw your tiny form,
and never held you, small and warm,
    within our arms,
    safe from all harm.
But you were our child,
  little one loved.

Little one loved,
  but loved by God far more than we,
and so He took you home to be
    with Him to stay.
    You went away
and left us grieving here,
  little one loved.

Little one loved,
  we wish you could have stayed with us,
but God is asking for our trust.
    Sometimes we cry;
    we question why.
To us, you'll always be
  our little one loved...

Our little one...
    gone home.

And now my soul is poured out upon me;
the days of affliction have taken hold upon me. Job 30:16

Staring sightlessly
    into the gray nothingness
        outside my kitchen window,
  I nurse a cold cup of coffee
    and brood over my listless soul.
The day stretches before me;
    an eternity of tasks
      awaits my unwilling hands.
There is nothing,
      nothing,
        nothing,
          alive in me;
I care for nothing,
      nothing,
        nothing,
          beyond that reality.
I am broken and empty;
    my soul is a shattered cup
      unable to hold joy.
    I am numb,
  numb with the nothingness
      within me.

In One Night

Arise, cry out in the night: in the beginning of the watches pour out thine heart like water before the face of the Lord: lift up thy hands toward him for the life of thy young children… Lamentations 2:19a

It was only a photo
        of a little family,
   but I stopped
      and looked closer.
Their son was nearly two
     by now;
   in fact, his birthday
      would be in a few weeks.
How could I forget?
   He was born
     that same night…

         and I remembered…

Hospital smells
   and hushed noises
     floated in the open door;
   my mom stood by my bedside,
       his mom at the foot,
     concern and caring
      etched on their faces.
Last night
   was a blur of faces and frantic activity,
      the emergency room,
        the operating room,
      the recovery room,
        all behind me
   as professionals dealt
     with the aftermath
      of our baby's departure.
I was empty
   of so much,
        empty of life,
     empty of hope,
        empty of emotion.

It wasn't really happening to me;
surely this was all a dream.

And then the curtain opened
to my husband,
a strange look on his face
as he came to my side.
"Give us a moment."
When we were alone,
he took my hand
and told me what he had just found out.
Last night,
down the hall,
a friend's child was born,
healthy,
crying,
alive.
And we wept
at the great unfairness of it all.
Even as a surgeon
removed all evidence
of our baby's life,
another doctor delivered
someone else's child
into their arms.
We had nothing.
They had everything.
We clung together
as reality struck us both.

Just down the hall,
they held their baby,
their hearts full
of nothing but joy.
Right there in that room,
we let go of a cherished dream,
our hearts full
of nothing but pain.

A Chapter of Pain

As thou knowest not what is the way of the spirit,
nor how the bones do grow in the womb of her that is with child:
even so thou knowest not the works of God who maketh all. Ecclesiastes 11:5

I did not know
  the absence of someone
    could be so great,
      so life-changingly sad.
It's the absence of someone
  who barely got to be,
    yet that tiny heart
      forever changed my world.

I did not know
  I would be called
    to stay behind
    and let go.
Oh, I did not know
  when first I learned
    of a tiny existence
      that life could be so fragile.

In that little life's coming…
    and going…
  in this difficult chapter of pain,
    I have learned more
    than I thought I needed to know.

The Pain of Letting Go

...my soul shall weep in secret places... Jeremiah 13:17

I see them everywhere –
  babies
    and the babies that will be.
It breaks my heart;
   the hollowness within
        grows hot with tears.
I touch the curve
     of a baby's cheek
   and think of one
           that's out of reach.

Oh, Lord,
       how can I find
      the strength to let go
          of a little one
    who died before
        he had the chance
      to even live?

Due Date

Are not five sparrows sold for two farthings, and not one of them
is forgotten before God? But even the very hairs of your head
are all numbered. Fear not therefore: ye are of more value
than many sparrows. Luke 12:6-7

My sweet baby,
  it hurts knowing that
    with the sunset of this day,
    your final chapter of life is written.
This is the day
    you were scheduled to arrive,
    but you came far too soon to stay.

My heart aches
    with the pain of allowing
  my baby to become
      nothing more than a memory.
It feels like betrayal
      to pack up those shattered dreams
  and open the new ones
            waiting for us.

Why should my child be forgotten?
        Is not even a sparrow
          due the notice of the Father?
Sweet child, I will always remember
    your short stay with us —
      as long as I live,
    you will not be one of the forgotten.

Dear God, forgive me.
    I know You hold my baby's soul
  close to Your heart,
        preserved for all eternity.
I just fear the thought
    of letting go and moving on,
            for it closes the door
        between me and my child.

I must let go. I must move on.
    Ahead there awaits
a brand new little life
      and new untarnished dreams.

Know this, Dear One:
    the pain of knowing you will fade,
but the anticipation of meeting you
      grows brighter every day.

Dear Baby

My times are in thy hand… Psalm 31:15a

I love you.
  Can you feel that love
     from way up there?
There's a lot of distance
   between there and here.
You will forever be
   the baby I lost,
  even though you dwell safely in glory
     as a completed soul
    with a full earth-journey behind you.
   Your times are in God's hands.
Your brief presence here
    was enough in God's eyes
   so He took you home.
Still, I go on loving you
   and wishing you had been asked
      to stay here a little longer.
You dwell, complete,
   a finished soul for His kingdom;
I go on, a piece of me gone.
  A bit of love
      has followed you,
  and I feel the emptiness
    left behind.
I love you,
   dear Baby.
I hope you know how much
   you are wanted and missed.
Don't let it make you sad.
   I'm coming by to see you someday.
    Until then,
I send you hugs and kisses
   and lots and lots of love.

   Love,
   Mommy

Child of Eternity

And this is the promise that he hath promised us, even eternal life. 1 John 2:25

I will always remember
          the thrill of knowing you were with us;
I will never forget
      the agony of letting you go back
           to the God Who made you.

I will always remember
          the anticipation of your arrival
      and wide-awake nights of dreaming;
I will never forget
          the pain of your absence
      and long midnight hours full of tossings and tears.

I will always remember
          the good and bad times that bearing you brought.
I will never forget…you,
          sweet child of fragile dreams and broken hearts.

Your brief presence has left
          indelible marks
              upon my soul.

I go on, picking up new hopes and dreams,
          looking into the sunrise of a new little life.
But I hope you know, little one,
          I will always remember…
              I will never forget…
                  you.

You are forever in my heart,
          my Child of Eternity.

Thoughts & Prayers

New Life

Thou hast granted me life and favour,

and thy visitation hath preserved my spirit.

Job 10:12

the joy and fear of life after death

Our hearts were broken by the loss of our first child, but a man's heart and a woman's heart have different rates of healing where miscarriage is concerned. My husband was very sympathetic and loving through it all, but he moved on into the next phase of healing much more quickly than I. He was ready to hold a baby of his own long before I was ready to even think about being pregnant again. I had been physically and emotionally drained by our first attempt at child-bearing; I feared knowing that kind of loss again. I wanted a baby, but I did not want to be pregnant. However, you can't have one without the other, so I laid aside the worst of my fears and committed our future to the Lord's care.

Four months after my hospital stay, I was pregnant...and happy...and scared. My emotions were on a roller coaster ride. I was just beginning to gain momentum in my anticipation and joy, when once more, I began bleeding. I cannot describe the sheer terror I felt. Happiness turned to dust in my mouth. I was sure we had lost this baby, too. I refused to hope. Last time I had hoped, and the devastation of loss was made much more painful by that hope.

I wasn't prepared to hear good news. That in itself was a shock. I asked the woman performing the ultrasound, "Are you sure? There really is a heartbeat?" And we looked and saw and marveled at God's goodness. This time I could go home and be pregnant.

But the bleeding continued on and off for six weeks as before. I lived from day to day wondering if this would be the last day for my baby. I prayed and cried and hoped and prayed. And I wrote, of the child I still missed and the child that, Lord willing, grew and stretched within me. There was comfort in committing my hopes and my pain to the Lord through paper and pen.

At the end of those six weeks, the bleeding stopped. Our baby lived, and shortly after that, little kicks allowed me to keep track of the life that thrived inside. Other complications developed, but there was life in there. My sore ribs gave daily witness to that fact.

A little over a year after our hopes and dreams were dashed, we held our precious daughter in wonder and joy. She was perfect, precious, a miracle straight from our heavenly Father. Our joy was complete.

The Question

Oh that I might have my request; and that God would grant me the thing that I long for! Job 6:8

We asked for a baby
      and received...
            a grave.
We asked for life
      and received...
            death.
We asked for a new beginning
      and received...
            a cruel ending.
We asked for joy
      and received...
            tears.
We asked for hope
      and received...
            only pain.
We asked if this was Your will
      and received...
            "Yes."
We submit ourselves
      to Your sovereign plan.

But, Lord,
      what will happen if we ask again?

Try Again?

Hope deferred maketh the heart sick:
but when the desire cometh, it is a tree of life.
Proverbs 13:12

Try again?
  My heart wrenches at
      his words.
He wants a baby;
    he wants me to want one, too.
      I do,
          I do;
    but here I sit,
        trembling inside
      at the thought of trying again.

Try again?
  Babies shouldn't be
      an assignment gone wrong,
          a redo –
        an erased mistake
            painstakingly reworked.
They should effortlessly awake
      beneath their mother's heart
  in the sweet afterglow of love.
A little heart should quietly find its rhythm
    and thump out its promise of life
            to come,
                to stay.
    We shouldn't have to "try."

Try again?
  My arms were left as empty
      as my womb
        when all that was hope
    escaped this harsh reality
          to flee into eternity,
      leaving me behind
  to put the pieces

back together.
I fear another new beginning
in the echo of such
a painful ending.

Try again?
How could we wish
to open ourselves
to the possibility of pain?
But we do,
we do.
We long to hold the child of our union
and our love,
and so...
we try again.

And effortlessly,
our daughter awakes
beneath my heart,
and hope dawns in our souls.
And this time,
a little heart keeps beating...
beating...
beating...
because we dared to hope,
we dared to dream,
we dared to try again.

Throughout the various experiences and difficulties that child-bearing brought to us, I have endeavored to find blessings amid the pain. Although our dreams were crushed by miscarriage, we have been so grateful that we do not have to face the additional pain of infertility. We also did not face numerous, subsequent miscarriages. When we dared to try again, we quickly saw the fulfillment of our desire for a child. In writing this poem, I am not trying to say those unable to conceive and bear children easily, or not at all, are not trying hard enough. I was simply remembering the walking-off-a-cliff sensation of a pregnancy after miscarriage. To those whose journey includes infertility or repeated miscarriages, my heart goes out to you. I cannot imagine your pain. May God bless you with grace and strength to face what life has given you to bear.

Changes

Now the God of hope fill you with all joy and peace in believing, that ye may abound in hope, through the power of the Holy Ghost. Romans 15:13

The rhythms of my body have changed.
The last time this happened,
I brought a child into this world…
but far too soon.
And now,
one broken heart,
one vanished little life later,
I recognize the signs
and know only fear.
Where is the hope,
the laughter,
the tears of joy?
How sad it is
to greet impending motherhood
with such emptiness.
I am afraid to hope.
Last time,
I lost myself to hopes and dreams.
Now I am simply lost.
I do not know for sure yet
if my intuition is right.
I'm not sure I want to know,
because then I would have to
deal with the knowing.
Does life exist
where death occurred?
I have lost a portion
of my innocence
in the devastation of my loss.
Grief has left
dark fingerprints on my heart.
Dare I hope?
Dare I dream?
I don't want to be
shattered all over again.

My Plea

Hear my prayer, O LORD, give ear to my supplications: in thy faithfulness answer me, and in thy righteousness. Psalm 143:1

Sweet new beginning,
      little promise of hope,
you are a beacon of light,
         a brand new start…
but please stay here;
     don't break my heart.

I fear the love
    I feel for you;
  it makes me so vulnerable
        to such a fragile being.
Oh, please stay here.
       Shine on, sweet sunbeam.

There was another,
      oh, such a little one,
who fled my womb
      much too soon.
So please stay here.
      Don't leave me alone.

I didn't know an absence
      could so totally break
         my mother-heart;
  it's hard to hope again.
If you stay here,
     maybe,
my broken heart will mend.

The Roller Coaster

There is no fear in love; but perfect love casteth out fear: because fear hath torment.
He that feareth is not made perfect in love. 1 John 4:18

I'm angry,
        Lord.
I'm angry
        and afraid.
It's an awful combination
    of emotions
        to feel on this
            advent of revelation.
There is a child
                within me,
            resting quietly;
    there is a presence
            unknown to all
        but us.
It makes me angry
    that my strongest emotion
            is fear.
Why should this child be deprived
        of anticipation?
Why should I have to wonder
    if this child will stay with us?
Oh,
    to know again
        the joy of being
                pregnant
            without fear!
And yet,
    You say
    perfect love casts out fear.
        I don't understand that.
I just wish I would know
        what will come of this child
    so I could prepare myself
            for the joy or grief
                that lies ahead.

I am angry,
     because I should know
          only happiness,
                    but I don't.
I am afraid,
          Lord,
     afraid of hope,
          afraid of love,
     afraid of what the future
          holds,
afraid to anticipate
     a child
     I may never
               hold.

Another Goodbye?

Is his mercy clean gone for ever? doth his promise fail for evermore?
Psalm 77:8

Little one,
　　you gave us such hope
　　　　at the promise of your coming.
Despite the fears
　　　　I had inside,
　　I was so happy
　you were on the way
　　　　to us,
　　　　　　to our home,
　　　　　to our love.

But now...
　　　　will the unthinkable
　　　　　happen twice?
Has your little life slipped away
　　　　so soon?
What can I do
　　　to provide a safe haven
　　　　　for my babies to grow?
　　What is wrong with me?
Will we never hold
　　　a child of our very own?

God,
　　　am I standing
　　　　　on the verge
　　　　　　　of another goodbye?

Miracle

I will praise thee; for I am fearfully and wonderfully made:
marvellous are thy works; and that my soul knoweth right well. Psalm 139:14

Sweetheart,
you move so strongly within me,
and I close my eyes,
confronted by the responsibility
of carrying a miracle inside.
It is one thing to marvel
at a blazing sunset,
a falling star,
the ripening buds of spring…
but it is another thing
altogether
to place my hand
over your questing toes
and know that I was created
to sustain this life;
and you were created
to depend on me.
You share my breath,
my sustenance,
my blood,
my life.
You are a part of me,
and yet,
you are no one but yourself.
You are proof to me
that miracles exist.
You are life
and promise
and hope.
You are my little miracle,
sweet baby.

Wonder

And God saw every thing that he had made, and, behold, it was very good...
Genesis 1:31a

It is a wonder
  to feel life within
      and to know
    this smallest of God's creation
        is dependent on you
        for life and love and laughter.

It is no wonder
  that God looked down
      at His created world
    and said of life,
        "It is very good."
New life *is* so very, very good.

It is a wonder
  to know that life
  has been created by love;
      just as God in His love
    brought life to this world,
  so our love has made life.

It is no wonder
  that God would give all
      to restore a broken world
    and a shattered relationship;
  we were created to be
      dependent on Him for everything.

It is a wonder
    the depth of love I feel
      for this tiny being.
Every movement
      is a reminder that life,
  small and helpless, thrives within.

It is no wonder
  that God loves us so much –
    He made us.
This little one, made of our love,
  is infinitely precious
    to my mother-heart.

It is a wonder
  that others can bring a child
into this world and not see God
    in this matchless creation
      of life and love.
The heart of God is seen in new life.

Child Birth

A woman when she is in travail hath sorrow, because her hour is come:
but as soon as she is delivered of the child, she remembereth no more
the anguish, for joy that a [child] is born into the world. John 16:21

Oh, the pain!
   The awful, overwhelming,
         all-encompassing pain!
It permeates my entire being,
      burning in every cell of my body.
There is nothing…there is no one,
               but me and the pain.
Surely I will die,
      and I'm not sure if I care.

Then…
      a freefall plunge into sudden joy!
               It's a girl!
She cries indignantly,
      and we laugh incredulously,
      sure that she is the most perfect daughter
               to ever grace this earth.
         And the pain is second
               to the joy.
It is a miracle to bring
         a child into this world.
Nothing is impossible
   in the wake of our accomplishment.
      We float in the effervescence
         of wonder and delight.
Thank You, Lord, oh, thank You
         for this child!

There was no place for memories
         in that room so packed with joy and promise.
But later, much later,
      I remember all the pain of heart and body
               that another baby brought.

Such empty pain and empty arms,
        hollow soul and broken heart.

Lord,
    bringing a child into this world
        was the hardest thing I've ever done
                except…
            sending a child to Heaven.

Close Call

The Spirit of God hath made me,
and the breath of the Almighty hath given me life. Job 33:4

We almost never met you,
　　　　Tiny One,
　　　my newborn daughter in my arms.

We almost never loved you,
　　　　Sweet One.
　　　We came so close to never
　　　　　　　seeing your first smile.

We almost didn't know you,
　　　　Little One.
　　A year ago,
　　　if our wishes had come true,
　　　　　　you wouldn't be here today.

We almost never held you,
　　　　Precious One,
　　　because our longing for another
　　　　　was far greater than
　　　　　　　the future's hazy promise of you.

We almost never named you,
　　　　Dear One,
　　　　　our Jenica,*
　　　because we serve a gracious God.

We were so blind, we could not see
　　　that He knew
　　　　　the plans drawn up for us,
　　and He didn't want us to miss
　　　　　the wonderful blessing of you.

You see,
　　　　there was another one,
　　perhaps a daughter or a son,

who wasn't born to stay here
in this world.
Had that baby lived,
dear girl,
you never would have drawn a breath
or known of life
here on this earth.
Our heavenly Father saw all this
and knew
we couldn't miss
the joy of knowing you.

Jenica means God has been gracious

Firstborn

...the firstborn of thy sons shalt thou give unto me. Exodus 22:29b

I go through each day,
busy with diapers and feedings,
naps and playtime,
holding my precious child
close to my heart,
lost to the miracle and effort
of motherhood.
Rarely do thoughts
of another little one
in a heavenly Father's arms
cross my mind.

But there is a time
when I always remember,
a time when the memory
of what was lost arises
with faded pain still marking it.

I am asked so often,
"Is this your first child?"
and I remember.

This sweet baby in my arms
is not our first,
will never truly be our firstborn.
There is a tiny soul who went
to live with God,
a tiny heartbeat
that inexplicably stopped beating.
Our firstborn.

Others forget.
A mother never does.

But why should I resurrect old pain
before strangers who are making
casual conversation?

My heart gives a little twinge
                of remembered loss.

          I reply,
"Yes, this is our first."
              The first child we got to keep;
          the first child we rocked to sleep;
                    the first child who smiled and laughed
          as we blundered through parenthood.

I don't tell them
          we started our family in heaven.
It is enough to remember.

Slow Learners

Lead me in thy truth, and teach me: for thou art the God of my salvation;
on thee do I wait all the day. Psalm 25:5

It happens every day.
She wants it,
begs for it,
cries for it;
I deny her the privilege of having it.
She thinks she has the right
to possess what she desires.
As her mother,
I know best.
I know some things could
hurt her;
Some things could cause
more harm than good;
Some things she is not
responsible enough to have.
I intervene,
and her little heart is broken
once again.
She is so sure
she knows
what is best for her,
but she doesn't.
It is a lesson
taught over and over
in the little schoolroom
of this home.
It is a lesson
she is slow to learn.

Today,
I was thinking of this
when I realized:
You are my Father;
You know what is best
for me.

You are the Master Teacher;
    I am Your beloved Slow Learner.

Help me,
    Father,
  to allow Your lessons,
    Your rearrangement of my dreams,
  Your firm, but gentle teaching
        to sink in.

We are,
    all of us,
        Slow Learners.

Tucked In

I will instruct thee and teach thee in the way which thou shalt go:
I will guide thee with mine eye. Psalm 32:8

I watched you sleep tonight,
    your innocent-unknowing
        caught in the dim light
  from the hall.
I studied your features,
    your sweet face
      turned toward
  a dream world known
        only to you.

Suddenly I was on my knees,
    driven by the overwhelming.
How can I,
    weak woman that I am,
  raise you,
    a precious soul straight from God,
   in such a way that you
      will learn to love
    the One from Whom you came?
I want to stand
    before the throne
      someday,
      knowing I have done
        all I could;
  who can do more?

I bow my head,
    internal tears
      streaming down my heart.
"Oh, God, help me.
    Help us
      raise her
        for You."
And you sleep on,
    unaware
  of whispers in the night.

Soon,
        I know the peace of surrender
                to the One who holds us
                        snugly tucked
                        within His mighty hand;
        who can know more?

You stir;
        I wonder
                if you feel
                the Presence,
                        too.

Thoughts & Prayers

The Thing Which I Greatly Feared

For the thing which I greatly feared is come upon me,

and that which I was afraid of is come unto me.

Job 3:25

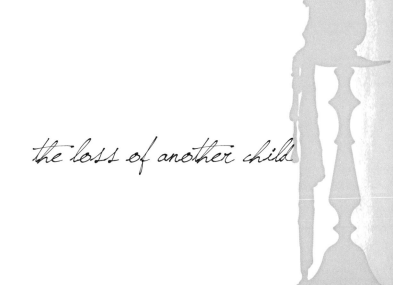

the loss of another child

Our life was complete…for a time. After a while, we became aware that our little girl would enjoy having a sibling almost as much as we would enjoy welcoming another child into our world. There was room for more joy in this little family. I feared pregnancy, with the rocky beginnings that seemed to be my lot, but we held the proof that my body was capable of bringing forth life. The reality of another child was starting to look possible when I began bleeding. This time it was a textbook miscarriage, over and done almost effortlessly.

Did that make it easier? Yes. Did having a child to love and hold make it easier? Yes. Did less time to wait and wonder about the outcome make it easier? Yes.

Easier, but still, not easy. I was unprepared for the journey that followed. With my first miscarriage, I came home from the hospital completely drained of all physical and emotional strength. I expected to feel badly, so it was no surprise when I did. This second experience was different because, while there were no extreme physical repercussions, the ongoing emotional effects continued to catch me off guard.

As I write this, two months after our second loss, I wonder how tomorrow will go. Sometimes I am unable to see past the pain of losing another child; the next day, I find pieces of hope to cling to and enough strength to consider the future. Our daughter has been a joy and a distraction to me while I am struggling to accept that another baby is gone. My husband is loving and very supportive, but understands this recent loss even less then the first, since I miscarried with little fuss or fanfare. Emergency room visits tend to clarify the reality of miscarriage. However, he has been very patient with me as I find my way back from grieving.

I still fear pregnancy. I fear I shall have to say good-bye to another child. I wonder why other women so easily acquire that which I cannot take for granted. When I see another woman with that glow, that walk, that glorious swelling of life – all the trappings of pregnancy – a twisting pain seizes my inner core, and I look away. *Oh, Lord, let me be one of those women again.*

I believe He will. I believe I will successfully bear another child to join our little family. But sometimes the fear of failure is stronger than my fragile faith.

The Secret

*Finally, brethren, pray for us, that the word of the LORD may
have free course, and be glorified... 2 Thessalonians 3:1*

It was our secret,
    brand-new,
      and we hoarded it to ourselves.
This time we would keep it
      just for the two of us a little while;
     this time it would be
        different.
Someday soon,
  we would jump up and say,
      "We're having a baby!"
    but not yet.
We would keep it
  a secret,
  and everything
    would be just fine.
But things went wrong,
  and the pain of carrying
    the unknown future alone
  was greater than
    the joy of surprising
      everyone.
    So we let our secret out.
We told the ones
  who should know
    that all may not be well,
     but we don't know
      for sure.
  Just pray.
Ask God that we may be able
  to bear whatever
    He has for us.

We're no longer hoping
  to keep our secret.
We're simply hoping
  to keep our baby.

Valley of the Shadow

Yea, though I walk through the valley of the shadow of death,
I will fear no evil: for thou art with me;
thy rod and thy staff they comfort me. Psalm 23:4

God,
   I cannot,
      cannot,
         cannot
     walk this road again.
Who do You think
     I am,
   that I can take again
    such heartbreak
        as I felt before?
Please,
      I beg You,
     let this nightmare cease;
       awake me
      from this awful sleep!
Surely You did not intend
    for me to face this pain again.
Surely You did not
      map this path
   for me to take.
     I must have turned wrong.
Show me the way back,
    out of this dreadful wilderness
        of loss.
You could not expect me
    to walk through
   this valley of the shadow
     of death
    all over again.

But looking behind me,
   there is no way
   to tell where I walked
        yesterday.
It is wilderness

all around me,
and no path
but the one
that lies before
my frightened feet.

How could this be
what You desire for me?
What plan do You have
that could include
this?

Then,
a Hand takes mine
and leads me forward.

Now I see.

You do not expect me to walk
through this valley of the shadow
of death...
alone.

I see, too,
the bloodstained footprints
marking the path ahead.
You've been down this road
before,
yet still,
You walk it once again...

with me.

Metamorphosis

...and we shall be changed. 1 Corinthians 15:52b

You flew away,
    but far too soon.
  You fled your
      tiny, warm cocoon
  for a better place,
      a warmer place;
  yet still I want you here with me,
    my baby butterfly.

Your feather touches
    go unfelt,
  by all but angels,
    who, I know,
  cannot help but love your gentle soul.
Oh, to be an angel
    and fly
      with my baby butterfly.

You were to stay
    and grace this dark world
  with the specialness
      that only you could give.
Your beauty and your spirit
    would have changed my world,
      but you flit among eternal flowers
    in Someone Else's world,
      my baby butterfly.

I would have held you,
    but, oh, so gently;
  I would have kept you,
    if only for a little while.
Perhaps you would have
      chosen to stay,
  but you were called,

and the compass in your soul
drew you inexorably
to your Eternal North,
my baby butterfly.

Do you not think
I cannot feel the pull,
made stronger
by your presence there?
And so you flew
into the great Unending Blue,
my baby butterfly.

Ah, sweet it is
to think of you,
drinking in eternal nectar,
soaring in celestial air,
lighting in the arms of our great Father.
But as I look
at the emptiness you left behind
in this cold, dark world,
I wish I, too,
could break loose of this
cocoon of humanity
and soar...

away...

away...

away...

to you and our great Father.

Someday,
I will be changed.
Someday,
I will know the metamorphosis of Heaven.
Someday,
I will fly with you.
Someday,
my baby butterfly.

Internal Propaganda

And ye shall know the truth, and the truth shall make you free. John 8:32

It just amazes me
　　how completely
　I insulated myself
　　from the reality of losing
　　　everything all over again.
　I had convinced myself
　　it couldn't,
　　　　shouldn't,
　　　wouldn't
　　happen to me again.
　I had talked my heart
　　　into believing
　　Death was unable
　to reach out and touch me
　　　once more.
Surely,
　everything would be fine
　　　from here.
　We had a child
　　running about,
　　　　getting into trouble
　　and our hearts
　with her winsome smile.
I was untouchable
　because my body had successfully
　borne life and love and laughter
　　into the sunshine of this world,
　　　and the world
　　was a better place for it.
So I talked;
　　　　so I believed.
When Death touched my womb again,
　the devastation was complete.

Lord,
　how can I find a new balance

between reality and hope?
How can I believe in new life
without an internal propaganda
of denial taking over?
How can I accept the truth
of miscarriage
without losing faith in new life?
I cannot tell myself that everything
will always go well,
but I cannot focus on how easily
life slips away from me.

Lord,
may Your words of truth and comfort
drown out the propaganda
that whispers in my heart.
Give me the strength to focus
only on You,
knowing that doing this
will make all else
fall into its proper place.

Misconception

Blessed are they that mourn: for they shall be comforted. Matthew 5:4

I thought it would be easier
  losing a baby
    when we already had one.

I thought it would be easier
  to let go of a dream
    when we still have one to cling to.

I thought it would be easier
  to accept this as God's will
    when He graciously has given one child to us.

I thought it would be easier
  to balance the pain and grief
    with the joy and love present in each day.

I thought it would be easier…
        it is…
      it isn't…
  and sometimes,
        it is again.

Our hearts are so full
    with the little blessing
  we've been given,
but somehow there is room –
      lots and lots of room –
  to love another.
Now that room has been emptied,
      and loss and sorrow
  rush in to crowd out what joy we had.

I thought it would be easier,
      and it is,
  because there are little hugs
      and silly grins

and childish games.
I am needed
        to be a mother
    to the child we have been given;
        it gives me less time
    to think about the child
            that has been taken.

And so,
        it is easier.

Yet still,
    the lament of loss echoes
        in the emptiness within me.

        I mourn.

Nothing can make that easier.

Surrender

Submit yourselves therefore to God. James 4:7a

I wept,
    and in the heavy stillness
        afterward,
I heard a whisper
    echo in the hollowness
      of my heart.
What are you willing to give up for Me?

"Everything, Lord."

    Silence.

He had said all He needed to say.

I wept again,
    but this time,
        tears of joy mingled
      with the pain.

Yesterday's Tears

I am weary of my crying: my throat is dried: mine eyes fail
while I wait for my God. Psalm 69:3

I cried myself out
  and dried my tears;
 I lifted my face to the sun
   and looked for a better day.
 I believed there was happiness
  waiting for me
  around tomorrow's corner.
My blessings surround me;
 my life overflows
  with far more than I deserve.
Surely I can be brave
 and put my grief behind me.
  So I believed.
I went into tomorrow with a smiling face.

So why am I crying yesterday's tears?
 Why am I broken again?
Why can't I find the end of my pain?
 Why am I crying the tears I cried yesterday?

I'm not a coward;
  there's not much that scares me,
 but this brokenness has shaken me
   to my core.
 I no longer know who I am anymore.
This loss has engraven
  its scars on my soul.
 I grope in the darkness
  that closes out the sunshine I crave.
I was going to be so brave.

So why am I crying yesterday's tears?
 Why am I broken again?
Why can't I find the end of my pain?
 Why am I crying the tears I cried yesterday?

Relapse

Oh that I were as in months past, as in the days when God preserved me;
when his candle shined upon my head, and when by his light
I walked through darkness. Job 29:2-3

The tears keep
    falling…
        falling…
            falling…
My heart keeps
    calling…
        calling…
            calling…
      for the sun,
    for the light to shine again.

But I'm lost in this darkness,
    blinded by my pain;
I can't see the path ahead
    for the tears that fall like rain.

I thought the worst was over,
    but it rises up to take control
and seize the tender, healing wounds;
    I'm bleeding, crying, heart and soul.

I thought the light had come to stay,
    that nothing could chase it away;
but now I'm lonely, lost, and scared,
    sure that no one knows or cares.

How can this be
    happening to me
        again?
I dealt with
    the worst of it,
        but somehow it came back again.

God, send the sun.
	End the rain.
Please,
	give me peace with my pain.

I am the supplicant;
	You are the Holy One.
This relapse has rebroken me;
	please, God, send the sun.

Recurrence

...I have lost my children, and am desolate... Isaiah 49:21

Maybe it was the music
    playing softly in the background.
   Maybe it was reading over the words
      penned in my moments of deepest pain.
  Maybe it was the reality and finality
   of what heaven now holds.

I cried;
    tears streamed down my cheeks,
      falling on the pages I had written,
        blurring the words,
  but not the awful truth.

There are two babies
     I have never held;
there are two wonderful children
    I can only love from a million miles
      and an eternity away.

Why does pain come back
   to strike at the most unexpected
    of times?
 It is these episodes
    that hurt the greatest.
Time lulls me into believing
  the worst of my grief
    is behind me.
 Oh, how wrong
     I can be!

God,
   comfort me...
    hold me.
     I am alone in my grief.
There is no one else
  who feels the loss

of my babies
as I do.
Life continues as it was,
the world not even noticing
the absence
of two precious souls.
Family and friends
have shown they care,
but still,
I cry alone.
It is so sad
that two of my children
have no one
to remember them with tears
but me.

But then,
Heaven is the greatest consolation
to earth's regrets.
My babies lack nothing and no one
Over There.
They have no need of me,
their mother,
in the presence of their heavenly Father.
Even that thought hurts.
All babies should need
a mother.

God,
comfort me…
hold me.
I'm crying again.

Retreat

*...when I fall, I shall arise; when I sit in darkness,
the* LORD *shall be a light unto me. Micah 7:8b*

I ventured forth
  from my place of pain,
      fortified, strong again,
    ready to face
tomorrow's arrival.
I had wept;
    I had mourned our loss;
    I had carefully packed
      another broken dream
          into Eternity's treasure chest.
      Heaven holds yet another reason
          to attend that final meeting in the sky.
But life goes on down here,
    and I was ready to deal with it
        again.

I ventured forth
  with my healing heart
    and spoke to others
  of the gift of pain.
It had been so very hard,
    but God was, as always,
    faithful in His care.
  Somehow, I found the strength
    to dream again
        after the tears,
    my rainbow of promise
      shining in the mist of loss.
I believed
    my heart was safely
        out of pain's grasp.

I ventured forth,
  with brand-new courage
    and then,
  today confronted me

with all its reminders
of what was so irrevocably
lost to me.
With brutal swiftness,
the healing is undone.
I am as weak and broken as ever I was.
My wounds are opened;
My heart is bleeding dry.

I retreat.
I can do nothing else.

I retreat
into this place of pain,
this place where healing
will happen again,
this place of honest words
and fragile hearts,
where darkness struggles
against the light of hope.
The light will win,
as it did before,
but today,
there is sweet refuge
in admitting I'm in pain.
There is an honesty
in the darkness
that is hidden in the light.
I see my vulnerability,
my weakness,
when surrounded by the night.
There is no place
for the trappings of pride and false courage
in this place of pain.
It is only me and my loss,
me and my God,

and I know Who will win.
Soon,
    I will return.
    I will venture forth
        from this place of pain again.
But today, I retreat,
    for I am not so strong
        after all.

Till Death Do Us Part

Many waters cannot quench love, neither can the floods drown it.

Song of Solomon 8:7a

facing loss together alone

When my husband and I vowed before the Lord "till death do us part," I considered only the very vague possibility that someday in the distant future one of us might be forced to live on without the other. But as we worked through the pain and recovery of miscarriage, I began to see another application for these words.

It has been our experience that a man and a woman respond very differently to the loss of a child through miscarriage. For my husband, the baby was a concept, not yet a reality. He was waiting to feel kicks and thumps, to see physical evidence of the life we created. I was a mother from conception, but the realization of fatherhood is less defined. I do not fault him for this; he has been created to use facts, not feelings, to relate to life and its difficulties.

Initially, we both mourned our loss. However, it became complicated when I was still grieving our child's death, and he was beginning to wonder when I would ever be "normal" again. This is when I found miscarriage to be such a quiet, lonely grief. Even the man I loved, the father of our child, did not completely understand my pain. He was loving, supportive, and very gentle with my broken heart, but he didn't *understand*. My grief drove a wedge into our relationship, parting two hearts that should have been united.

Time is our God's gentle salve for grief. The days and weeks passed, and we were able to find each other again as we reached out across the distance that stood between us. We are closer now, our relationship stronger for having suffered pain and loss. But we will always remember the terrible solitude of those days as we both looked to the other for something we were not able to give.

A Man of Strength

Two are better than one; because they have a good reward
for their labour. For if they fall, the one will lift up his fellow:
but woe to him that is alone when he falleth;
for he hath not another to help him up. Ecclesiastes 4:9-10

Thank You, Lord,
    for this man You have given me.
Thank You for his strength
      when I have none.
He's hurting, too,
    but he doesn't wear it on his sleeve.
  He has shed tears, too,
      and, Lord, I know this is
  a disappointment to him,
      but thank You for his strength.
Thank You that he can help me move on.

He doesn't express his emotions
    like I do.
He doesn't seem to be grieving our loss –
    he is,
      but he's a man,
  and You made him to be strong.
Lord, help me not to resent
    his acceptance of our baby's death.
Instead, help me to lean on the strength
    of that acceptance,
  to look outside my walls of grief
    and see the world –
  a world he wants to share with me.

Lord, help me to see
    how much he needs his loving wife
  that's lost right now
    beneath a grieving mother.
Thank You, Lord, for this man.
  He's strong enough
    for both of us right now.

The Stranger

And she was in bitterness of soul... 1Samuel 1:10a

Who is this woman
            I've become?
In the last half hour,
      I've snapped at my husband,
            slammed a cupboard door,
                  muttered under my breath,
      scowled and griped and frowned.
If there were a mirror in this kitchen,
      there'd be a stranger
                  staring back at me.

Who have I become?
      This is not the woman
            I remember:
                  the glowing, blushing bride,
            the loving, supportive wife,
      the ecstatic mother-to-be.
This is not the woman
      he remembers either.
I see that knowledge
                  in his eyes,
            and it burns me
      to my soul.

Who is this woman
            I've become?
I thought I accepted
            our loss, our pain;
      I thought I'd worked through
            the emptiness within me.
But now I see
      the emptiness is gone,
            because
      (oh, God, can it be true?)
I have become a woman
      filled with bitterness.

A Husband's Plea

Then said Elkanah her husband to her, Hannah, why weepest thou?
and why eatest thou not? and why is thy heart grieved?
am not I better to thee than ten sons? 1 Samuel 1:8

"I miss you," he said.
     "How could you miss me? I'm right here."
"You left me," he said.
     Tears stung my eyes. "I'm trying to come back."

I went away.
          I'm sorry.
     I did not know I was gone from you.
My mind and heart were absent
               as I attended the graveside
                    of another lost child.
It is a place
          that exists only for me,
     in the deepest regions of my heart.
I did not realize
          you felt my retreat
               to this place of grief.
I knew only
               that life had ended
          where all should have been beginning,
     and if I didn't mourn
               the passing of a little soul,
                         who would?
Do not blame me, please.
     I know I've been distracted,
                         tired,
                              hurting.
Now you're hurting, too,
          because you are missing your wife.
It was wrong of me to forget you.
          I'm sorry.

I'm coming back,
          and this time,
               I'll try to stay.

Our Loss

Woe is me for my hurt! my wound is grievous:
but I said, Truly this is a grief, and I must bear it…
my children are gone forth of me, and they are not… Jeremiah 10:19-20

Does he look at me
        and wish I were another?
Does he wish as much as I
        that I could effortlessly
                carry our children
                        into this world?

Instead of being
        a fountain of life,
    I have become a funeral pyre
            on which two have been borne
                    into eternity.

It aches to know
        a child is ushered away
    because I have failed…
                                again.

My head knows
        there is nothing
        I could have done differently.
    I cannot blame myself
                for that which is
        beyond my control.

My heart knows only
        another child is gone.

When I see
        the safe haven
    other women create
            for their babies,
        the pain runs deep,
                out of reach
                        of words or comfort.

He says no words of blame.

He tries to comfort
        in that awkward, uncertain way
                of a man confronted by a grief
        he does not understand.

But I wonder,
        does he long
        for things to be different?
Does he want me
        to just forget about our loss
                and move easily on?

Sometimes
        the deepest pain
        is in the simple truth
                that *our* loss
                is really *my* loss,
        in oh,
                so
                        many
                                ways.

Grief Process

They who have loved together have been drawn close;
they who have struggled together are forever linked;
but they who have suffered together have known
the most sacred bond of all. -Anonymous

It worries him when I am sad.
    Grief is an intangible
        that he can't fix.
There is no reality to our loss
      for him.
The pregnancy had not become
    a child to him;
      it was too soon for him to know
        the truth in bulges and kicks.
And so,
    he cannot understand my preoccupation
      with the emptiness within.
He assures me there will be another child
    to love and hold someday,
      but he can't see
  how the promise of tomorrow
    doesn't heal the pain of today.

He deals in facts;
    I am pure emotion.
He faces reality head-on;
    my feelings are the filter through which I look at life.
He sees the possibilities;
    I focus on what lies beyond my reach.
He wants life to go on as before;
    I am sure it will never be the same.

We are two opposites,
    and it is never so obvious
  as when we face change, loss, and grief.

He is loving,
    but he does not understand.

He is sympathetic,
      but he doesn't know what to say.
He wants to go on as normal,
        but I cannot.
    There is something in me missing
        that he wants back,
     but I no longer can find it.

    Someday I will again.

Until then,
    it is balm to my soul
  to know he will still be here
      when I come back
 from laying yet another child
        into the Father's arms.

Thoughts & Prayers

A Community of Shared Pain

Blessed be God, even the Father of our Lord Jesus Christ,

the Father of mercies, and the God of all comfort;

who comforteth us in all our tribulation,

that we may be able to comfort them which are in any trouble,

by the comfort wherewith we ourselves are comforted of God.

2 Corinthians 1:3-4

the sisterhood of travail

Miscarriage can be an incredibly lonely experience for a woman. Often, she is the only one who felt any strong emotional attachment to her baby, especially if the miscarriage occurs in the early weeks of pregnancy. Her husband may not be able to identify with her feelings of loss and emptiness. Her friends may be ill at ease and reluctant to discuss something so personal. The sad truth about miscarriage is that the only way to really understand its effects is to experience it.

It is at a time like this that she may become aware there is a community of women whose common bond is miscarriage. Many of these women are willing to help another woman through her loss and grief. To share pain is to lighten the burden of it. No one in this sisterhood of travail needs to feel alone.

I was blessed with the presence of many women in my life who could identify with my sorrow. They offered words of sympathy and the light of hope and healing when I was lost in the darkness. My prayer is that you, too, can know the gift of shared pain.

Receiving this gift created in me a desire to pass on what had been so graciously given to me. It also made me more aware of the pain and heartaches of those around me, especially if it was caused by our common enemy: miscarriage. The poems in the following collection were created from my observations of and interactions with other women, as they shared in my journey and I in theirs.

There are several poems included here about my conversations with those who have never had a miscarriage. These poems are a compilation of events and are not based on one situation or person alone. Many women, in their earnest desire to say something comforting, can unfortunately say the wrong thing. It is not my intention to accuse anyone of being unkind. I, too, have said unintentionally hurtful words to someone whose experience and grief were different than mine. We mean well in our efforts to comfort, but grieving hearts are tender hearts and so easily bruised.

I believe that miscarriage should not be swept under the rug and ignored. Different women react in various ways due to the circumstances of the miscarriage and their own emotional makeup; however, there still needs to be recognition of the loss as a child. To say it was "just a miscarriage" is to undermine the sanctity of life. According to God's Word, every unborn baby is a living soul from the moment of conception. (Psalm 139:13-16) You have an opportunity to stand for truth in a degenerate world by admitting to the death of your child and your quiet grief.

Allow yourself an appropriate time to grieve, then look for an opportunity to be used of God to touch someone else's wounded heart. Your new and hard-earned knowledge of this unique loss can minister to another woman's pain. You may be the light God uses to guide her in the darkness.

Let Me Hold Your Baby

Be merciful unto me, O God, be merciful unto me:
for my soul trusteth in thee: yea, in the shadow of thy wings
will I make my refuge, until these calamities be overpast. Psalm 57:1

Let me hold your baby –
and grieve the loss of one
whom His Father took before
I could take him in my arms.

Let me hold your baby –
and – just for a moment – pretend
that yours is mine and grief is gone
and everything's all right again.

Let me hold your baby –
let me cry these tears of loss.
It hurts, it hurts, to be the one
who has to count death's painful cost.

Let me hold your baby –
let me feel the mother-love inside.
She is not mine, but let her bring
a memory of one who died.

Let me hold your baby –
I know you do not understand.
Just for a moment, let me cry
when little fingers clutch my hand.

Soon after my first miscarriage, I visited a friend with a small
baby. I hoped that holding a baby would help to fill the emptiness
*inside me, but it didn't work. I wanted **my** baby.*

Regrets

Comfort ye, comfort ye my people, saith your God. Isaiah 40:1

Not too long ago,
        you lost a baby, my friend,
    before he even had a chance
        to taste of life.
I heard of it and thought
            that I should call you –
    but what would I say?
How do you comfort a woman
        who has lost someone
    so intimately connected to her
            and her alone?

So I didn't call.
        Now I regret it.
Now I know that it doesn't really matter
            what you say,
        but that you cared enough
    to step out of your own experience
            and express your grief
                    for someone else's loss.
Now I know that a woman
        just needs to hear
    that someone is remembering
        there was a little presence within her
            that is no more –
    that someone is hurting with her.

I didn't call.
        I didn't know what to say.

Now I do.
        I lost a baby, too.

Heartbeat

And the LORD, he it is that doth go before thee;
he will be with thee, he will not fail thee, neither forsake thee:
fear not, neither be dismayed. Deuteronomy 31:8

You carry in your womb
　　　a tender promise,
　　such sweet possibility.
A soul rests gently
　　　in your care,
　　a tiny being
　　　destined to be a part of you
　　　　　for always.
Yet you stand hesitating
　　　　on the edge of anticipation
　　because there was another…
　　　　another tender promise,
　　　　　another sweet possibility,
　　　　another tiny soul
　　　that now knows only Jesus' care.
How easy it's become to fear.
　　　　Your hope,
　　　　　　your heart,
　　　　　your dream
　　　was crushed
　　and left you trembling
　　　　　in its wake.
How hard it is to hope again,
　　　　to dream of possibilities.
　　　Life is much more fragile
　　　　　in your eyes
　　than it ever was before.
Death has rendered you afraid
　　　to immerse yourself in joy.

Ah, sweet mother,
　　　know this with all your heart –
　　the same Jesus
Who holds your broken promise,
　　　your tiny dream,

the little life that ended
                    far too soon,
        is holding you
    and this new little promise
                    in His arms.
Lay aside your fears,
                your pain,
            your worry —
    and rest in Him.
He has given you
            new life to bear.
Take up your happiness
                and walk,
        secure in the knowledge
        that God has you and yours
                    in His care.

This was written for a friend whose first pregnancy ended in miscarriage. During her second pregnancy, she admitted to me that she lived in fear it would happen again. Not too long after, I discovered that it was one thing to write these words and quite another to believe them in my heart.

What Do You Do?

He hath shewed thee, O man, what is good;
and what doth the LORD require of thee, but to do justly,
and to love mercy, and to walk humbly with thy God? Micah 6:8

What do you do
>>> when your heart is broken in so many pieces,
>> and you can't find the strength
> to pick them up
>> and start over?

What do you do
>>> when there are babies everywhere,
>> except in your empty, empty aching arms?

What do you do
>>> when the pain within is stronger
>>> than anything else in your life,
> and you are simply overwhelmed by it?

What do you do
>>> when you can't see beyond yesterday
>> and can no longer dream
>>> of a brand new tomorrow?

What do you do
>>> when everything you planned and hoped for
>>>> is gone,
>>> and you are left behind
>> to make sense of the impossible?

What do you do
>>> when life as you have always known it
>>>> has ended,
>> and you have become
>>>> someone new…
>>> and shattered…
>>>> and changed?

What do you do
    when loss has etched itself into the window
        of your soul,
  and you look out through it
      into a world that is harsh...
        and cold...
    and cruel?

What do you do
    when you come to the end of yourself
  and find nothing to cling to,
        nothing to depend on?

What do you do
    when through your pain,
      God speaks to you,
  and you realize your response to suffering
  will forever change who you are
          and why you are?

What do you do?...
    take one day at a time...
    cling to the Lord...
  spend time with those you love...
      look for others who need you...
  learn to dream again...

And even though you never thought
    you would again,
  you will live,
    you will love,
      you will laugh,
  and life will be sweet once more.

My Apology

Set a watch, O LORD, before my mouth; keep the door of my lips.
Psalm 141:3

Oh, God,
   I did not know,
      I did not know!
   That I –
knowing the pain of careless words –
      should drive them deep
         into another heart!

I did not mean to,
   but that doesn't change her tears,
      doesn't give her
      what she so desperately
         longs for.
I thought I had heard
   she carried another child,
               but she doesn't;
   the pain in her eyes
      and the tears she shed
               are hot coals
         burning my heart.

I am so sorry,
      but I fear
   what lingers in her heart
      is not my apology.

I do not know
   the deep, deep pain
   of longing…
         longing…
            longing…
as yet another month goes by,
      and flowers lay over the grassy cradle
         of an only child.

I know but a little of her pain,
    enough to lie awake
and remember
    the words
I never should have said.

I pray God
    she is not doing
        the same.

Well-Meant

Now the God of patience and consolation grant you to be likeminded
one toward another according to Christ Jesus. Romans 15:5

Why do some people
        feel obligated to point out
    that there are many others
           who have lost much more than me?
Are you saying that I have no right to grieve
      because you have weighed my loss against theirs
            and found mine wanting?

It is salt in my wounds
        to be reminded that I am not
    the only one who suffers.
I know that, but right now
             I am hurting.
It takes time to mourn,
         time to heal,
     time to see beyond my own pain.
I'm still working on it.
  It does not feel good
        to be told I could have lost more.
It feels even worse
      to have examples of greater sorrow and grief
        held up before me
   as proof that what I am going through
     isn't so very terrible after all.

Maybe I am taking too long
     to snap out of it.
Being with you
    makes me believe
     you think
   I should just get over it.
But at the moment,
        my broken heart
  is more real to me
     than the comfort you are offering.

I won't tell you this.
I won't hold your words against you.

You mean well,
        and right now,
    my heart is too easily bruised.

But in my short walk of pain,
        I have found the most comfort
    in a friend's silent tears
            when she heard our baby was gone.

Sometimes tears speak louder than words
                and offer far more consolation.

Weep With Them That Weep

Rejoice with them that do rejoice, and weep with them that weep.
Romans 12:15

Don't speak to me
of hope and opportunity;
don't tell me that tomorrow
holds new dreams.
I am not done dealing
with the grief today has brought;
I have not buried all the pain
within a brand new grave.
My loss is far too real
to think that someday
it will fade;
my life is in too many pieces
to believe that
it will ever be made whole.
I cannot see beyond today,
so don't bring up the future.
It is no consolation to hear
my sorrow will be forgotten.
Don't pat my shoulder
and say that there will be another child;
that comfort brings no light
into the darkness of my grief.
Don't belittle my loss
by forcing me to look into the future;
my eyes are so clouded with tears and pain
I can barely look into your face.
But your words will echo in my hollow heart,
and though I know that you mean well,
I see clearly you do not understand.
You've never lost a child in this way.
Maybe that's what it takes
to know the words to say:
"I'm sorry."

Please…
weep with them that weep.

Chance Encounter

For we walk by faith, not by sight. 2 Corinthians 5:7

We met,
  and I could barely meet her eyes,
    unable to face the reality of my pain.
She came down the hall
  at the midwife's office
      with that classic rolling gait
    of a pregnancy in full sail.
She didn't have long to wait
  to hold her little one,
    but I…
  I would wait until forever
    to see my baby.
My hand went to the empty flatness
  which should have been swelling slightly
    over my baby's resting place,
      but no…
    my baby rested
        in the arms of God.

It wasn't fair,
    and I watched her secretly.
  It hurt, it hurt to see her so,
      but I could barely look away.
Why, God, why me?
    Why did you take my baby home
        while so many stay and thrive?
She has a houseful already;
            I have none.
It isn't fair,
      isn't fair,
          isn't fair.

And not so long from then,
  she bore a son, her second one,
      and their world was complete.

I grew strong enough for us to try again,
and one year later,
God gave us a little girl,
and it was very good.

Time passed,
and her world fell apart.

We met,
and I could barely meet her eyes,
unable to face the reality of her pain.
We came through the line
to where she sat,
next to the tiny casket
cradling her son, too young to die.
She held him, loved him,
cherished him for two short years,
but now her baby rested
in the arms of God.

And I…
I hid my face in the sweetness
of my daughter's hair.
It isn't fair,
isn't fair,
isn't fair.

She lost her son
after months of fighting and praying,
gaining ground against the cancer,
then losing all in so short a time.
I couldn't help but think
of our meeting long ago,
and how I envied her.

Her houseful is missing one now.

We both were called
        to give our babies up
    to Your all-knowing plan.

Perhaps I did not lose so much,
        because my child never drew a breath,
    but I mourned alone,
        and my child is…
                forgotten.

No mother wants her child to be forgotten.

Perhaps she did not lose so much,
    because she has precious memories
        of smiles, laughter, and love in the midst of pain.

But, oh, the empty place left behind
            is so much larger.

Oh, Lord,
    how could I know
        in that first encounter
  what You had in store for us?
We both have lost,
    but, Lord,
  we know Who holds our babies now.

Hold us, too, Lord,
    when heaven seems to be
        an eternity away.

The Pool of Siloam

And [Jesus] said unto him, Go, wash in the pool of Siloam, (which is by interpretation, Sent.) He went his way therefore, and washed, and came seeing. John 9:7

Cry…
    for you have lost
        that which you never
            will regain.

Weep…
    for all the mother-love
        inside that has no place
            to go.

Grieve…
    for your brand-new joy
        that has been twisted grotesquely
            into pain.

Mourn…
    for all the should-have-beens
        swept away in a sea of tears
            and life-blood.

Sorrow…
    for many do not understand
        and will not remember your broken heart
            and lost child.

Cry…
            Weep…
        Grieve…
                Mourn…
        Sorrow…
    and then arise…
                Go…
Wash in the pool of Siloam,

and you will see...

The Living One
    Who holds your child
            in His hands...

The Healing One
    Who knows your broken heart
            and longs to comfort you...

The Loving One
    Who once gave His only Son away
        and knows the pain you're feeling now.

And with new eyes,
            perhaps someday,
    the memory of the pain you know today
                will allow you
            to offer hope and help
        to someone who gropes along
            the darkened path of grief
                    on their way
                to the pool of Siloam.

Jesus told His disciples that the man blind from birth was born sightless so that "the works of God should be made manifest in him." Sometimes God asks us to go through grief and loss in order to work in and through our pain. I dedicate this poem to those of you who have lost your first child to miscarriage. With no other little one of your own to hold, you bear an extra burden of loneliness and uncertainty about the future. May God give you the grace and strength to accept this loss and someday... God willing...to try again. I also pray that you will find it in your heart to reach out in love to someone else who is blinded by pain.

The Hypocrite

Let the words of my mouth, and the meditation of my heart,
be acceptable in thy sight, O LORD, my strength, and my redeemer. Psalm 19:14

God,
      how can it happen twice?
    Do You wish to remind me
          of my loss?
   I was doing so well,
          and then,
     the news came.
She carries a child
   whom she will hold
      while my arms are still empty.
With no fuss or bother,
      she harbors life,
    but I…
I still grieve
   the departure of another little promise.

The greatest portion
   of my pain
     is that this has happened before
       to the two of us.
We are not in a race,
       a contest,
    or a game of achievement.
She didn't set out
    to show me up.
This is nobody's fault.
    I know that –
  underneath the pain.
It is just so unfair
   that I have no guarantee
   of life
with each new baby.

I do not wish this pain
     upon her.

I do not want to make her
            feel guilty.

So somehow,
        I will need to find
    the courage to look her in the eyes
        and wish her the best,
            even while I am shedding
                tears of grief and…
                            yes…
                                anger…
                    inside.

God,
        if hypocrisy is
            saying one thing and feeling another,
        then I could be
                the most hypocritical
            of all women.

Help me,
            God.
    Help me believe in my heart
        that this is all part of Your plan,
            and therefore,
                    it is good.
    Help me truly want
                the best for her
        and rejoice with her,
            even though I carry
                only tears
                    within me.

From One Mother to Another

Wait on the LORD: be of good courage, and he shall strengthen
thine heart: wait, I say, on the LORD. Psalm 27:14

Not so long ago,
    I stood where you stand today,
        watching someone else's baby
  in someone else's arms
      and feeling the pain
          burrow a little deeper
             into my heart.
My brave smile
    felt broken and brittle
        at the edges
  for the memories
    of what could have been,
      should have been,
        mine.
My soul was bent
    beneath the weight
      of a thousand shattered dreams.

Now today,
  I stand here with my arms
      as full as my heart,
  with joy and hope
    and warm pink blankets.
I look at you,
    and I remember the pain.
A tiny measure of guilt
    rises up to shadow
  the rosy promise I live in today.
It is not fair
  that I should so quickly
    see the fulfillment
  of a dream that once was crushed.
It is not fair
  that I should stand here
    with my baby,

and you stand there...
            without.

My heart breaks for you
            even as I admire your courage.

There is nothing so brave
            as a childless mother
      smiling into the eyes
                  of someone else's baby.

The Elephant in the Nursery

Even when I remember I am afraid, and trembling
taketh hold on my flesh. Job 21:6

It looms,
           larger than life,
      and we spend most of our time
             trying not to see it.
I know it's there;
                    you know it's there;
      we all see it and look away
                because,
                              well,
         what is there to say?
My miscarriage has become
             the elephant in the nursery.

It trumpets,
           louder than words,
      and we try not to hear
                 the echo of pain.
You carry a child;
                 I carried a child;
      we both know
         it should have been different,
                          but it isn't.
You will labor to bring forth life;
         I will labor to hide my tears
      as you bring in yet another miracle.
My heart has been trampled
           by the elephant in the nursery.

It lingers,
           longer than memory,
      and we move on
         with our busy lives.
Some of us will forget;
                 some will never forget;
      those of us that have lost
           feel its presence wherever we go.

But it takes on new and fearful dimensions
as you bring your sweet newborn in,
and we gather around to marvel,
peering past
the elephant in the nursery.

*The phrase "elephant in the room" refers to an obvious issue or truth that no
one wants to address or discuss. Miscarriage is often the elephant in the room
because it is such a private grief suffered by one individual. Other women may
know about it, but feel awkward about introducing the topic. The grieving mother
doesn't always have the words or the composure to bring it into conversation.
(I personally feared that others would think I talked about it too much.)
This poem first formed in my mind as I stood in the church nursery watching
a friend holding a brand new baby in the middle of an admiring crowd.*

Conversation

Bear ye one another's burdens, and so fulfil the law of Christ. Galations 6:2

Please talk to me.
        Don't look away and start discussing weather.
My life has not ended
        with the death of my baby.
    I need to know you remember I'm grieving,
            although I am trying to move on.
I never had the chance
        to hold my baby as you hold yours;
        there are no words to say how much that hurts.
I know you feel ill at ease –
        I did, too, not so long ago.
How do you ask a woman
        who has just lost a tiny little miracle
            how she is doing?
There are tears,
                and grief,
            and pain,
        and an emptiness within,
                    so vast,
    so immeasurable –
        words are not enough.
But talk to me anyway.
        Ask me how I've been
            so I can say
        I'm doing better than I was
                yesterday
        and tomorrow,
                maybe,
        I will be able to say the same.
The pain isn't over;
        the tears are not done.
    Still, life must go on,
            even when a tiny one has ended.
You say you don't understand,
        and perhaps you don't,
                but talk to me.
I need your help to move on.

Have Compassion and Help Us

…if thou canst do any thing, have compassion on us, and help us.

Mark 9:22b

the gift of comfort

My friend had a miscarriage.

What can I do?

⤷ Ask God for wisdom and words before you approach her. God will provide your need as you minister to hers.

⤷ Ask her how she is, how she is feeling, and how you can help. Listen to her answers without forming quick responses in your mind while she is speaking.

⤷ Lay aside your own beliefs and thoughts on miscarriage. This is not about you; it is about her and a baby she longs to hold, but cannot.

⤷ Make a note on your calendar when her due date would have been and send her a card on that day.

⤷ Give her a small gift or flowers in remembrance of the little life that is gone.

⤷ Cry with her. Your tears are an indication of your caring far above what you might say.

⤷ If her first pregnancy ended in miscarriage, her house may seem especially empty to her in the days ahead. Stay available for her to depend on for company or phone calls.

⤷ Send her a Mother's Day card, *especially* if it was her first pregnancy. Although she does not hold a baby in her arms, she is still a mother. That recognition of her status is incredibly special to her.

⤷ Pray for her. Although you can do much, she has wounds only God can truly heal. She needs your prayer support more than anything else. Tell her that you're praying for her. That in itself will be a comfort.

⤷ Be careful. You are spending time with a fragile heart.

⤷ Avoid any statement that begins with "at least". For example, I have heard said, "At least you weren't very far along." "At least your baby is in heaven." "At least you have two children." When the words "at least" are used, it makes it sound as if it could be a lot worse. Perhaps it could be worse, but a mother who miscarried a baby she loved and anticipated is struggling to accept a very painful reality. Don't make light of her pain by using the words "at least."

≈ REALIZE THAT IF you are pregnant, this is probably not the best time to actively reach out to her. The physical reminder of her loss that you carry with you may speak much louder than any words of comfort you offer. A woman who has recently miscarried finds it painful to spend time with pregnant women. A card, note, or phone call may be the best option for you.

≈ IT IS EASY to tell her that you thought about calling her, but never got around to it. That's taking the easy way out, trying to assure her that she's not forgotten without having to spend the time and effort it would take to pick up the phone or write a note. If you didn't get it done last week, don't tell her about it. Do it today.

≈ SHOW INTEREST IN her as an individual, not just as a "miscarrier."

≈ REMAIN CONSISTENT WITH your relationship prior to the miscarriage. If you spent a lot of time together, don't drop out of her life now. If you aren't very close to each other, don't choose this experience as an opportunity to become "best friends." Keep the expression of your sympathy in proportion to the depth of your relationship.

Things you should not do:

≈ DO NOT JUDGE her if she doesn't act as you think a bereaved woman should. Be flexible and noncritical. Different women grieve in different ways.

≈ DO NOT FORCE yourself into her life if she needs time and space to heal. If she doesn't want to talk about it, be sensitive to her reticence.

≈ DO NOT TELL others what she may confide in you privately. If you are not sure, ask her what she considers too personal to share if someone would come to you and ask about her.

≈ DO NOT COMPARE her situation with your cousin's wife, who lost two babies at birth, which surely, you think, must be worse than one miscarriage. Don't talk about your sister-in-law who can't get pregnant at all. Don't talk about anyone else. You are there for her. To compare her loss with others who are "worse off" appears as if you are minimizing her grief. These are NOT words of comfort; they are words of pain.

- DO NOT SAY that the baby probably had something wrong with it. You don't know that, and it provides no consolation to her.

- DO NOT TELL her that she'll get over it once she gets pregnant again. That is not the case. While the pain may be lessened by the joy of another baby, the miscarried baby lives on in the mother's heart.

- DO NOT TELL her to call you if she needs anything. She probably won't call. Tell her you'll bring supper tomorrow night, or invite her and her husband over for an evening, or go on a walk with her on a sunny afternoon. Being specific with your offer shows the depth of your sincerity. A vague offer of help is often someone trying to express sympathy without expending too much effort.

- DO NOT PITY her. Encourage her – carefully – to get back on her feet emotionally. It may take some time before she will be ready to hear this, so be wise in choosing your moment. If you provide only pity, she may continue in the cycle of grief without ever realizing it is time to break out of it.

A list of *Do nots* is a bit intimidating.
Let me add one *Do not* as an encouragement:

- DO NOT LET your fear of saying the wrong thing keep you from saying anything. Perhaps after reading some of the poems in the previous section, you may wonder if there is anything you can say that won't hurt or offend a woman in this situation. If you approach a woman about her loss with love and concern in your heart, your caring will shine through whatever words you chose to say. Keep it simple; keep it sympathetic.

God bless you as you give of yourself in this way. It is a priceless gift of love you can grant to another woman in pain.

Mourning All the Day Long

I am troubled; I am bowed down greatly;

I go mourning all the day long. Psalm 38:6

washing my dishes in tears

When your heart has been broken, the routine duties of the day can trigger sudden emotional crises. Washing dishes or folding laundry can suddenly become tearful and traumatic. How do you deal with the pain of everyday life?

Your life needs to have purpose and meaning beyond the grief you are experiencing. Grieving is good, healthy, and normal, but your life did not end with the death of your baby. Find a reason to get up in the morning by pouring your heart and soul into something meaningful to you. If it's writing, then write. If it's tackling that project you've been putting off, then tackle. If it's housecleaning all your closets, then houseclean. If it's doing something for somebody else, what are you waiting for? Keep busy, even though you have to pause to dry your tears.

You do these things, not to escape your pain, but to work through it. Beware of any activity that blocks your ability to process your emotions. There are many entertainment options in today's world that shut your mind down. Filling your head with enough "noise" to drown out your pain only delays the inevitable. Allow yourself to grieve, but don't stop living your life as God intends you to live it.

There are many beneficial activities that will help you move through the grieving and recovery process, but it is God Who does the true work of healing in your heart. Go boldly to the throne of grace in your "time of need." Talk to God about your pain. Spend time with His Word. I frequently read and reread the Psalms, many of which are the prayers of David. I also found comfort in the Gospels, especially when I saw again the love and compassion Jesus had on the people He walked with each day. There is healing in the heart of Jesus. He expended great time and effort into making the wounded ones whole. It was a great comfort to know He cared just as much about my broken heart.

Your child would not want you to spend the rest of your life caged by your grief or guilt. You will find joy again, and when you do, you will discover that the deeper tones of your tears and sorrow have created a lovely harmony with the lighter notes of laughter and happiness. Your joy is so much sweeter after the pain.

Empty Promises

For, lo, the winter is past, the rain is over and gone;
The flowers appear on the earth; the time of the singing of birds
is come, and the voice of the turtle[dove] is heard in our land.
Song of Solomon 2:11-12

Staring out my bedroom window,
   I see buds adorning all the branches.
      The daffodils are opening,
    spreading yellow petals to the sun.
  The grass is green;
       the peepers chant their mating cry;
    the robin's calling fills the sky;
       the creatures know that Spring's arrived;
  but I...
    I cry.
I cannot face a sun that laughs
    without asking why it does.
All the earth is shining,
        reaching,
    growing,
  except the hollow place
       beneath my hand
  where once my baby was.

Overwhelmed

...put thou my tears into thy bottle: are they not in thy book? Psalm 56:8b

They said I would feel sad,
    maybe not want to eat,
  or be with people,
    or do anything.
They called it depression.
  It's baby blues
    with a razor-sharp edge,
  for there is no baby to hold.
    I said I was fine.
My family was supporting me,
    and I could laugh through my tears,
  and talk through my grief,
    and be with those I loved the most.
I honestly thought I would be fine.

    That was last week.

Today, I am sad.
  I don't feel like eating,
    or being with people,
    or doing anything.
My heart is an open wound,
    and I am bleeding my pain
    everywhere.
There is a bottle of tears,
    so fragile, so full, so nearly broken,
      just beneath a tender surface.
I am scraped raw,
    exposed,
      hurting.
I don't know how much of this
    my wounded heart can take.

    This is today.
I don't know if I can make it
  to tomorrow.

Phone Call

The LORD is good, a strong hold in the day of trouble;
and he knoweth them that trust in him. Nahum 1:7

She called me before the news was out;
              for that I guess I should be thankful.
    To have heard it from someone else
would have been terribly painful.
           But, God, it isn't even right!
    It is salt poured into an open wound.
Losing my baby is hard enough,
      but to watch the pregnancy of a friend?
And the hardest part of all is this:
             her due date, a week after mine…
    a week after mine would have been
      had my baby not inexplicably died.
She said she has heard the heartbeat,
      and my own heart wrenched at the words.
  My baby's heart had scarcely been beating
          when heaven's sweet calling was heard.
I told her I was happy for her
    though the words seemed to stick in my throat.
  We chatted of many and various things;
           my responses were chosen by rote.
And after good-byes, I hung up the phone
          and burst into thousands of tears.
I couldn't believe it; it hurt me so much,
    the dawn of my very worst fears.
To watch a good friend count down the days
      and anticipate holding her firstborn,
         when I could have been counting as well…
    it's just another reason to mourn.
God, why does she have to be bearing a child
    so close to the day I once longed for?
  My heart breaks again as the tears keep falling;
        I didn't know I could hurt this much more.
God, help me to smile when I next see her,
        and help me to carry this pain.
  May she never know this kind of loss,
        and help me find healing again.

Hope

And now, LORD, what wait I for? my hope is in thee. Psalm 39:7

"Look, there's another big rock."
My husband and I
were knee-deep in water,
braving the April chill of our creek.
An hour ago, I had received
a phone call from a good friend.
She was expecting their first child
and wanted to tell me personally.
Normally this would have been good news,
but my newly empty womb ached
with the absence of a little one
that had been scheduled for arrival
only a week before my friend's baby.
Oh, it hurt! And after countless tears,
I asked my husband if we could go
down to the creek and wade.
A week ago, we had started a dam,
just for fun and because we couldn't
when we were children,
and suddenly I felt the need to be
anywhere, but in the house
weeping over the sink of dish water,
trying not to think
about the might have beens.
And now, with the spring breeze in my face,
the brave sun waking up the earth,
and the laughter of the creek around my toes,
I felt I could catch my breath
and tuck a rock into the dam in my heart,
which held back a never-ending
supply of tears.
I placed a rock on the creek-dam
and reached for another.
Hopefully, someday, the warm sun
of time and healing will dry up

that vast reservoir of tears within me,
spilling over without notice
so often these days.
But until then, perhaps
one more rock in the creek-dam
will be one more rock
in my tear-dam.
My husband pulls me close
and gives me a long hug.
I look up into his eyes
and feel the warmth
of his love,
of the spring sunshine,
of a Father's care for a broken heart.
There are still tears that will be shed,
pain that lies ahead,
healing that hasn't happened yet.
But standing here, with the creek
wrapped around my feet,
healing seems Possible.
An hour ago, it didn't.
That's all I can ask for now.

God,
thank You for looking
out for me.
Thank You for giving me
Hope.

Child's Play

And the streets of the city shall be full of boys and girls
playing in the streets thereof. Zechariah 8:5

The laughter of children
    echoes in the spring air.

I watch them tumble on the lawn,
    without a fear, without a care.
  They just simply live and breathe
      in the moment, for the moment.
   I can't help but think
    of the child that was, but went.
I still stumble through the rubble
    of my dreams, my broken aftermath,
  and these children laughing in their play
     makes me want to hear my child laugh.
I'm sure my baby laughs
    in the shining glory air,
      but why should angels listen
    and not his mother? It's not fair.
My child's safe in Jesus' arms,
    and God's a gentle Father;
  but still, I long…
      I wish…
        I dream…
    a broken-hearted mother.

The children tumble past me,
    their laughter high and clear;
  I smile at their antics
     and brush away a tear.

My Prayer

Cause me to hear thy lovingkindness in the morning;
for in thee do I trust: cause me to know the way wherein I should walk;
for I lift up my soul unto thee. Psalm 143:8

Lord,
    give me faith to accept the shadows
          and the rain.
      Lord,
    give me joy when my heart
             is enmeshed in fear.
    Lord,
give me hope
      when the darkness deepens
          and hides my tentative dreams.
    Lord,
give me laughter to blend with my tears,
    creating harmony out of the discord of pain.
Lord,
      give me reminders
  of Your matchless grace and infinite love
    when it seems all grace and love have run dry.
      Lord,
    give me compassion when my heart is cold
        with disappointment and heartache;
        help me to see others' needs.

Lord,
    You have created me,
        a woman of such great needs,
      but You are the source of my help
         and the answer to my questions.
  You have created all things,
    so surely You can create
        a woman of God out of me.

Scrapbook

Be of good courage, and he shall strengthen your heart,
all ye that hope in the LORD. Psalm 31:24

I hold in my hands
               a million tears,
          a collection of pain,
                    an outpouring of hurt
          from those who have lost.
I am humbled by their pain.
          Who am I,
     that I would dare assume
          to set pen to paper
               and ink out my loss?
There are many who have lost
          so much more than I.
I turn pages of pain,
          words written when speech
                         was too hard,
          poems of heartache
     beyond spoken expression.
Who am I,
               to long for what was lost
          when another tiny miracle
                    lies hidden in my womb?
I have heard the sweet music
                    of a secret heartbeat;
     I have been given another dream,
                    another hope,
               another child.
Nothing will replace what was lost,
          but still,
          I am blessed.

And yet,
          in the silent night,
     in the stillness and shadows,
               when sleep will not come,
          I remember,

and the pain could not be greater.

There is a baby
        who knows only Jesus' arms;
    there is a child
        whom I have never held.
It is not fair to anyone
    to weigh pain against pain
            and find someone's wanting.
It does not matter
                how much you have lost,
        only that you have lost,
            and you are hurting.
There are many who care,
        and many of these people
            have lost as well.

God,
    I am humbled that You
        should think me worthy
    of joining the ranks
            of the healing ones,
        the ones who have loved and lost,
            and found hope again.
I am honored that You have wrought
        a great work of compassion in me
    through the death of my baby.
I commit my feeble efforts
            to Your guidance
    and ask that You help me
        use the memory of my pain
    to bring hope to those
who know what it is
        to lose a miracle
                to eternity.

Beneath the Pines

Thou shalt keep them, O LORD, thou shalt preserve them
from this generation for ever. Psalm 12:7

There is a quiet place,
                beneath pines and shadows,
        in a peaceful corner of the world.
There a dream lies hidden,
        cradled in the bosom of the forest floor.
It is a tiny piece of the terrestrial
                left here after the celestial flew home
        to be with the loving Father.
Oh, God, that our baby
        should come to this?
A tiny, tiny grave lies
        at the foot of a young pine tree.
No cold, hard stone
        to mark a painful absence,
    only the softness of pine needles
                and tender plants reaching to the sun.
    No fence is there to guard the place
        and keep it safe.
No name,
        no sign,
                no marker…
Will anyone remember
                after I am gone?
        But while I am here,
            I will remember.
While I am here,
        there will always be
                a tiny memory
        beneath the pines.

And someday, God,
        should You bless us,
    I want to sit in the warm grass
        and watch our children
            beneath the pines:
    the children that run,

and play,
and laugh,
and love,
and give such sweet joy with their life –
and the child that rests quietly
at the foot of a stately pine
and lives on,
in eternity
and in my heart.
As the children scamper
and romp in that friendly grove,
I want to remember
all that You have done
and keep on doing.
I want to know
that You hold all of us
in Your loving arms.

I want You to watch over
my children
beneath the pines.

Undone

Then said I, Woe is me! for I am undone... Isaiah 6:5a

I am a tree,
    stripped by the wind,
  naked, leafless in the cold,
        high upon the mountaintop,
     no shelter near
            and Spring so far.
I am a tree,
      trapped by Winter's unrelenting grasp,
   shivering and barely hanging on.

I am a house,
    once warm and welcoming,
  but now abandoned
      to Time's unforgiving hand.
    Empty eyes of broken glass
        stare out into Tomorrow,
   bleak and lonely,
      no longer loved, protected, cared for.
I am a house,
      left behind to fall apart
  and lose all sense of home.

I am a clock,
    wound down,
       silent on the wall,
     hands hanging uselessly,
      uncaring that Time still marches on.
Broken from within,
        its empty face
     reflects the shattered pieces
       in its heart.
I am a clock
     that lost all sense of purpose
   with the tragedy inside.

I am all things lost and lonely,
empty and broken,
poured out and useless,
shattered on the floor.
And it is now,
when even the strength
to rise up on my knees
is gone,
when my purpose,
my hope,
my work,
is done,
I hear Him say,
My purpose,
My hope,
My work,
has just begun.

Pain Speaks

Therefore my people shall know my name: therefore they shall know in that day that I am he that doth speak: behold, it is I. Isaiah 52:6

Pain speaks of mortality,
reality,
eternity.
Pain is unwelcomed,
unwanted,
undesired.
Pain has no expiration date.
It is bigger than I am.
It is stronger than I am.

Pain speaks of failure,
of heartache,
of loss.
Pain is the marble stone
bridging this world
and the next.
Pain holds the world at knifepoint.
It knows no boundaries.
It respects no guarded borders.

Pain speaks to kings,
to priests,
to common folk.
Pain is a curse,
a gift,
a chain.
Pain speaks of death and finality.
It is the slamming of a door.
It is the clunking of a lock.

Pain speaks…
Lord,
help us to listen,
for You so often can speak to us
through the words of Pain.

Haunted

The LORD redeemeth the soul of his servants:
and none of them that trust in him shall be desolate. Psalm 34:22

The unknowns
  haunt me,
sit on my shoulders
  and whisper
     of dreadful possibilities,
  mock me with glimpses
     of both hope and pain.

I could live
  with this weakness
    of my body
  if the results would not be
       death and tears.
I could bear
  the burden given to me
     if I would have the promise
       of a child in the end.

But I don't know,
  and some days
  it drives me
     to tears.
I battle with the lack
    of knowledge
  almost as much
    as the ultimate loss
      I have now
      known twice.

A Season of Dying

For my thoughts are not your thoughts, neither are your ways my ways,
saith the LORD. For as the heavens are higher than the earth,
so are my ways higher than your ways,
and my thoughts than your thoughts. Isaiah 55:8-9

Lord,
  I don't understand
      Your purpose here.
I am surrounded
    by heart-rending
        beauty,
      in flaming reds,
        smoldering oranges,
          and burning yellows.
This is autumn
    at its clearest,
        brightest best.

I could weep
        at this vibrant beauty.
I could weep
        for the next high wind
      that will effortlessly
        destroy this amazing display.
Why,
      God?
Why did You invest so much beauty
        into this,
      a season of dying?

Lord,
    I don't understand
        Your purpose here.
I am surrounded
      with such crystal clear evidence
          of Your love and caring
        for a hurting heart.
So seldom have I felt
      so close to You

or known the sweet trust
of depending on Your promises
to help me through
the pain in every day.

I could weep
at the clarity of Your love.
I could weep
at the nearness of Your presence.
I could weep
for the last high wind
that swept my child
away into eternity.
Why,
God?
Why do you invest so much beauty
into this,
a season of dying?

Falling Up

*The eternal God is thy refuge, and underneath are
the everlasting arms... Deuteronomy 33:27a*

Autumn sheds its splendor
    on the wind,
      each leaf a passing second
        on its dying face.
Falling...
      falling...
            falling...
                  all but one.
I saw today
  a leaf caught in the updraft
    above our little valley.
It soared up
    and up
      and up
  into the great blue arms of heaven,
    far above the twig
      on which it clung
    throughout Summer's bygone days.
It spiraled in the sun,
    falling up.

Lord,
    may I be as this little leaf
      and fly above the heartache
      and the pain that holds me down.

May I be as this little leaf,
  Lord,
                and up...
          and up...
      falling up...

        into Your great and gentle arms.

The Sleeping Monster

…ye approach this day unto battle against your enemies: let not your hearts faint, fear not, and do not tremble, neither be ye terrified because of them. Deuteronomy 20:3b

I tiptoe
    through the shadows of my soul,
        afraid lest I awake
        the fears and tears
        that lurk within the dark.

I have known joy,
        but not today;
I have known hope,
    but it is far from me
        in this black hour.

I do not know
    what lies ahead
        in wait for me.

I can only tiptoe
            and pray
    that fear will not
        awake today.

Moments

Blessed are they that do his commandments, that they may have right to
the tree of life, and may enter in through the gates into the city.
Revelation 22:14

It was a moment
  captured in the sunshine and laughter
 of a little girl
 and two puppies
  tumbling across the lawn.
  Unbidden
 came the thought:
  you should be here, too,
  in the sunshine and laughter.

It was a moment
  hidden deep in the night shadows
 as I tucked a blanket
 under a chubby chin,
  whispering lullabies to my baby.
  Unbidden
 came the thought:
  you should be here, too,
  in the night shadows.

It was a moment
  woven in the tapestry of my day.
 I watched her face
 as she discovered something new,
  and I knew wonder again.
  Unbidden
 came the thought:
  you should be here, too,
  in the tapestry of my days.

It was a moment
  encircled in the warmth of family.
 I sat beside my love
 and she played at our feet,
  and all was as it should be.

Unbidden
came the thought:
   you should be here, too,
   in the warmth of family.

These are the moments
         marking the passing of time.
   I am in the midst
      and whirl of life,
            when suddenly I think of you.
      Unbidden
   is this thought:
      you should be here, too.

But you are in a better place,
         and somehow,
   I imagine you standing,
            tiptoed and smiling,
      peering through a pearly portal
            between our world and yours.
You watch us
   in this harried, hurried life,
      and sometimes,
I think I hear you whisper,
      "Oh, Mommy,
            you should be Here, too."

Life Lessons

Thy hands have made me and fashioned me: give me understanding,
that I may learn thy commandments. Psalm 119:73

I have learned
>   death fears no one and no reason.

I have learned
>   pain can go deeper and reach farther than happiness.

I have learned
>   loss can rob you of one thing,
>   and, for the moment, it's everything.

I have learned
>   grief is a season of tears with no limits and no restrictions.

I have learned
>   smiles can be plastic masks worn over broken hearts.

I have learned
>   memories of what should have been
>   come to mind more easily
>   than those that have been.

I have learned
>   miscarriage is a quiet grief forgotten so easily...
>   by all but one.

I have learned
>   moments of joy in the midst of sorrow
>   are so much sweeter than everyday happiness.

I have learned
>   hugs will say some things words never could.

I have learned
>   hope is a rainbow, but sometimes the flood does return.

I have learned
>   babies come in three sizes:
>   small, medium, and heavenly.

I have learned
>   laughter is a skill that can be lost...
>   and found.

I have learned
>   God is greater and stronger to me in my pain
>   than in my joy.

Just Another Day

When I remember these things, I pour out my soul in me... Psalm 42:4

Inside out:
   my heart not only pinned
         onto my sleeve,
   but all over me –
         raw,
            exposed,
               vulnerable,
         with every event of today
   trampling on my emotions.

Today
         is just another day
      for everyone else.
Today
         is just another day of remembering
                  for me.
Sometimes that which lies
      in the past
            awakes to wander
   through my soul,
         and I am unable
      to stand before the onslaught.
My heart is felled;
      my emotions are tangled
         around that which
            barely got to be.

This day is yet another step
         in the winding, darkened
      staircase of healing
               up toward the light.

Today is just another day
            for everyone...
      including me
         and my memories.

Insomnia

When I lie down, I say, When shall I arise, and the night be gone?
and I am full of tossings to and fro unto the dawning of the day. Job 7:4

He lies beside me
    asleep;
I stare into the blackness
    awake.
I did not need this,
    this insomnia,
    to add to the crippling exhaustion
    I drag around with me
    every day.

Sleep!
Why can't I sleep?!
    It's what normal people do at night.
    As for me,
I've counted so many sheep
    they've started looking real enough
    to grow wool and have babies…

Babies…
    Other people can,
    and I didn't.
Why?
    What went wrong?

Why can't I sleep?

This wretched wakefulness
    has been my only companion
for far too many midnights lately.

He sleeps,
    and I don't.
Why does that make me angry?
    It isn't his fault.

None of this is his fault;
      it's mine,
    and my body that failed us.

I wish I could close my eyes
  and make it all go away
          for a little while.

I wish I could close my eyes
  and fall asleep…
       like him.
If wishes were horses…
     or maybe sheep,
  in this case…

I'm so tired.
    Why can't I sleep?

Anniversary

Because thou shalt forget thy misery, and remember it as waters that pass away. Job 11:16

I go through each day
　　unconscious of Time's relentless tread.
I simply live…I laugh…
　　　　I cry…I breathe;
　and moments pass,
　　　　turning into days
　　　　　　and weeks
　　　　　　　and months,
　　　　　and later still,
　　　　　　　　　to years.

I am surrounded
　　　by family,
　　by friends, by memories,
　　sheltered by it all.
Except when in its march
　　　Time brings an anniversary by,
　　and I remember
　　　　the once upon a time
　　that never found
　　　　　a happily ever after.
It's the story of a life
　　　　unbound by time,
　unhindered by memories,
　　　unknowing of the grief
　　　　　　left in its wake.
When I look at all
　　that lies between what was
　　　and what now so wonderfully is,
　　I realize,
　　　　to my surprise,
　　it happened quite a while ago.
Ah,
　but today…
　　　today,
　　it feels
　　　　like yesterday.

Dress of Hope

*It is good that a man should both hope and quietly wait
for the salvation of the LORD. Lamentations 3:26*

I spread the fabric;
    I lay out the pattern;
        I cut the pieces,
  large voluminous pieces,
suitable for a woman
      much more rotund
  than me.
I should be rotund;
    I should be round;
        I should be great with child,
    but I'm not.
  Still,
I cut out a dress,
  a maternity dress,
    a dress for a mother-to-be.
I will sew it together
  and hang it in my closet.
It is my dress of hope,
    my garment of promise,
  my reminder that miracles
      still happen every day.
Someday,
  that miracle
  might happen to me.

I will look at this dress
  and know that I still
    believe in hope.
Sometimes,
  I forget to believe.
Maybe if I see hope
  hanging in my closet,
    I will remember.

Pity Party

Look upon mine affliction and my pain; and forgive all my sins.
Psalm 25:18

What are You doing here,
        Lord?
  This table is clearly set
            for only one;
     this cup of tea,
          steeped in loneliness,
    isn't enough for two.
I didn't invite You
       to this party,
     because there is no room
        for Pity with You here.
  I didn't invite You,
       so why did You come?
I *want* to feel sorry for myself;
   I *want* to linger
     over my Pain and Grief.
  It isn't fair
     that Death has taken
       what should be mine.
It isn't right
   that life has given me
      pain, and not a child, to bear.
And You could have
  kept that pain away,
    but You didn't,
       so go away,
         Lord.
I don't want to hear
   those gentle reminders,
     those loving reassurances,
  those insistent encouragements
    to crawl out of my hole
    and move ahead in faith.
Do you know how hard this is,
       Lord?

Oh, that's right.
       You do.

I'm sorry,
       Lord.
Please forget what I just said
                     and come on in.
I'll pull up another chair
       and put on more water to boil.
    Just let me dump
          this cup of Pity.
It was getting cold,
              anyway.

Table for Two

And he was withdrawn from them about a stone's cast, and kneeled down, and prayed, saying, Father, If thou be willing, remove this cup from me: nevertheless not my will, but thine, be done. Luke 22:41-42

You crashed my pity party,
          Lord;
                    now what?
Your presence fills this small room;
          there is no room left for me
                    to focus on myself.
You have poured me
          a cup of Peace and Blessing,
                    and I see now
                    that I was wrong to dwell
                              upon my loss.
But,
          could You pass me
                    a little direction, please?
I am at a loss,
          Lord.
          It hasn't been all that easy lately.
I'm just a woman
          with all the emotions and feelings
                    that go with it.
Right now,
          those emotions are too much
                    for one woman to handle.
I should have called You sooner,
                    Lord,
          I know.
I've felt so overwhelmed
                              and lost
                    and scared
                              and…
                              angry.

I guess I needed to tell You that.
   I'm glad You're here;
I needed the company.
   I need You,
      Lord,
      to straighten out this mess
   I've made of my emotions
         and get me back to living
               for You.
Not for myself,
         Lord,
      but for You.

Yes, I'll take another cup, Lord.
      And the prayer that goes with it,
               Lord?
      Yes,
   I'll take that, too.

Not my will, but Thine, be done.

April in My Soul

The joy of our heart is ceased; our dance is turned into mourning.
Lamentations 5:15

It is winter,
 but within me, new life blooms,
 all the crocuses and daffodils
  of a thousand springs
  rising up beneath
   my glowing heart.
No bitter wind,
 no bruising cold
  can breach the warmth
   and happiness I feel.
Although the ice may cling
 tightly to the eaves,
 it cannot touch
  the April in my soul.

It is spring,
 but within me, the naked limbs
 of death and grief
  stand etched against
 the gray horizon
  of my heart.
An icy fist is clamped about my throat,
 choking off the hope and joy
  that once grew so fearlessly within.
My heart lies stripped
 of all the promises and dreams
 that flourished deep inside.
    All is silent, still, and cold.
It is spring,
 but there is no April in my soul.

Only Child

There is one alone, and there is not a second… Ecclesiastes 4:8a

She is older now,
    two and counting,
   talking and giving her opinion
     of the world
       in which she lives.
She is our joy
  and our challenge,
    and we love her
   more than words
     can say.
We had hoped
   she would be joined
  by a sister or a brother
     sometime this summer,
  but that child
    has gone to live
     with God.
I have learned to live
   with the pain
    of that truth.
I am learning, too,
    to live with the reality
      of the question:
   "Is she your only child?"
Oh,
   the pain of having
    a big sister
     that cannot hold
the baby that should have been.

There will be,
     God willing,
   another child,
  but there will always be
    a place left empty
     by our midsummer child.

Stick People

...for the memory of them is forgotten. Ecclesiastes 9:5b

She has discovered
　　the joys of pens and pencils.
　She gleefully makes her mark,
　　　a page full of scribbles.
Then her little hand
　　stuffs the pen into my own,
　　and she begs
　　　　for me to draw.
Indulgently,
　　　I make a little family,
　　stick figures with no life
　　　but that which shines in her eyes.
　　　Daddy...
　　　　　　Mommy...
　　　　　　　　　　Me!
　　　She snatches the pen
　　　　and colors them in.

Later,
　　　I find the paper family
　　and ponder on that hasty sketch.
　　　Suddenly,
　　　my eyes are filled with tears.

Oh, Lord,
　　there should be a little figure
　　　　here and here.
There are these spaces,
　　　　　empty places,
　　　where there should be smiling faces,
　　and no one ever sees them
　　　　but me.

Overprepared

*For that ye ought to say, If the LORD will, we shall live,
and do this, or that. James 4:15*

Last summer,
    I looked into the future
      and saw a baby
        that surely would be blessing us
          next year.
I canned and froze
    with a vengeance,
   putting up food
        that next summer
I would not be able to do
     with a new baby here
    or shortly to arrive.

Last summer,
   I planned for
     next year
    with an efficiency
  that today
    hurts me.

For a brief while,
    mid-summer bloomed
  with promise.
For a brief while,
    it looked like I had
   wisdom and foresight.

This summer,
   I will do my canning and my freezing –
     what little I shall need to do –
        as always.
This summer,
    I will know
  the pain of being
      overprepared.

A Small Triumph

And he said unto me, My grace is sufficient for thee:
for my strength is made perfect in weakness.
Most gladly therefore will I rather glory in my infirmities,
that the power of Christ may rest upon me. 2 Corinthians 12:9

Looking back,
    I can see the stain
of tears in the fabric
    of my heart. The pain
    has left its mark
in the very essence of my soul.
There are the scars
    of broken pieces somehow
made into a mended whole.
I see it all, the hurt,
    the loss of what can never be
    regained. My heart
quivers beneath the onslaught
    of the bitter memory.

Looking back,
    I see the strength won hard
in the trenches of my heart
    as I confronted the reality
of dreams that fell apart.
I see a work of compassion wrought
    within my life as I loved
and lost and let go.
It was a deadly battle fought
    and has etched its loss
    in the front lines of my soul.

But looking back,
    I see who I was
before and after,
    and I know in my soul,
although I would have chosen my life to be otherwise,
the pain of loss and shattered dreams
    has created in me
a woman of deeper strength and compassion.

Final Truth

Peace I leave with you, my peace I give unto you:
not as the world giveth, give I unto you.
Let not your heart be troubled, neither let it be afraid. John 14:27

Lord,
    life has turned out
        so differently
   from my dreams.
The cup of joy
    I held up to You
   has been filled with pain.
There have been shadows
     where I expected only sunlight;
   there has been weeping
     when I expected only a song.
I have walked through
   far too many valleys
     hidden in darkness and fear.
It seemed so pointless,
      so purposeless,
   to lead me down these paths.
How could You possibly
   receive any glory
     in this calling of loss?
    But as I emerged
      from the depths
    in which I had walked,
I began to see
   something I never saw before,
    something made clear
in the glorious light
    of Your love.
There is such peace
   in knowing this final truth:

You never waste my pain;
   You're using it to build
     something wonderful in me.
I'm learning that my pain

is part of the foundation
in the castle of my dreams.
And somehow in this journey,
there is joy among the tears,
for You'll redeem our suffering
after many years.

A Note from the Author

Shortly before Thanksgiving 2009, we welcomed another little girl into our family. We thanked God for her safe arrival; she was healthy and very vocal about the indignity of being born.

She made her entrance into this world via c-section. During the procedure, the surgeon confirmed our suspicions. I have a bicornuate uterus, which in layman's terms means I am heart-shaped where I should be pear-shaped. I did some research on this condition and found conflicting opinions on how much it causes miscarriage. According to one source, there is a 55-63% fetal survival rate with this condition, although another source I found suggested there was little correlation between the two. I suppose there will always be an element of the unknown with most early term miscarriages. One fact the sources agreed on was that the baby has a 50% chance of being in an abnormal presentation, such as tranverse or breech, which was the reason for my second delivery being a c-section. A bicornuate uterus is considered a birth defect, and there is no way to correct the condition.

Looking at our two daughters, we are aware of the sacredness and fragility of life. It is an incredible responsibility to raise these precious souls for the King.

If I could condense this book into one sentence, I think it would be: "Lord, use my pain for Your good." The conviction that there was a reason for my pain and my poems grew stronger over time. I was driven to compile my writings into this book by the belief that my pain will not be in vain. Somehow through my grief, God gave me words I can use to minister to another hurting soul. Somewhere there is a woman who has no words for her pain, and these poems may give her a voice. And so, with trembling hands and heart, I pen these closing words, for in giving you this book, I have ripped aside the curtains of my soul and allowed you to see deep within. I do it only because I believe God can use my pain.

—Stephanie J. Leinbach

The author lives in Blair County, Pennsylvania, with her husband, Linford, and two daughters, Jenica and Tarica. They attend Tyrone Mennonite Church, a recently established outreach congregation. In addition to writing, she enjoys reading, teaching, and creative challenges.

Poem Index

First lines in italics